Why Bad

Things Happen

Why Bad

Things Happen

_____

and what is our comfort

ARUNDEL PRESS
Mazeppa, Minnesota, USA

Copyright 2021
Published by Arundel Press
Michael S. Martin
43265 C.R. 83
Mazeppa, Minnesota 55956 USA
(507) 273-6107

For trade discounts or quantity purchases, contact the publisher.
Printed in the United States of America.

ISBN: 978-0-9883120-1-2

Scripture quotations are from the Authorized King James Version.

Acknowledgements

Thanks to God and His Son Jesus Christ, who will redeem us from all bad things.

Thanks to my wife, Brenda, for helping me to form and clarify these thoughts and for walking with me through the good things and bad things of life. Thanks to my children for enduring hours of table talk on this subject in the past decade.

Thank you, Brother Merle Ruth, for your close doctrinal scrutiny of this book. The hours we spent together discussing the manuscript were invaluable.

Thanks to my brothers and sisters in Christ for your meditations on Scripture, your discipleship, your stories, and your prayers. You contributed more than you know to these pages.

Editor: David L. Martin, Rochester, WA

Copyeditor: Melody Martin

Cover design: Brenda Martin

Cover photo: Taken near Long Creek, OR, by Stephanie Martin

Final design and typesetting: Theodore Yoder, Red Bluff, CA

Printing: Pilgrim Book Printing, Stoneboro, PA

Reviewers and Contributors:

Merle Ruth

William Child

Aden Gingerich

Samuel Coon

Virgil Schrock

Randall Plett

Timothy Kuepfer

Samuel Bauman

Paul Kaufman

Joshua Robertson

Philip Petre

Roger Berry

Kurt Morse

Harley Kauffman

Rodney Witmer

Jason Gingerich

Noah Miller, Jr.

Dean Rosenberry

Dale Martin

Bob Krause

John N. Miller

Troy Schrock

Dedicated to the memory of

Winston Blake Martin

My son

Linda Lou (Groff) Martin

My godly mother

John D. Kurtz

A dear friend and inspiring brother

all of whom are now beyond the reach of bad things.

Contents

Foreword

It has been one year since our oldest daughter's disappearance and death. The unimaginable has happened. Jeremiah asks, "Is there no balm in Gilead? Is there no physician there?" God knows that grief is a wound that takes time to heal. We are still in that process, but we thank our Father that we have a lively hope both in this life and in eternity.

We have wrestled with the issues addressed by this book and appreciate the answers given. The idea that God causes evil to happen because of some greater good that He is looking for is an idea that bears correction.

Where is God? Why? These questions surged over our storm-tossed vessel, threatening to sink our faith. Sometimes it has been hard to even think about hearing the Lord's voice, but He is there speaking above the wind and waves.

In Matthew 14 we read that Jesus sent the disciples across the sea. They obeyed Him, only to be caught in a fierce wind storm. Rowing hard in the dark against the churning seas until the wee hours of the morning, they were utterly exhausted with little hope of living until daybreak. When Jesus suddenly appeared, they cried out in fear. Then, He spoke through the howling wind and roaring waves.

"Be of good courage! It is I. Be not afraid."[1] No doubt the disciples wondered, "Are we hearing the voice of the Lord? Is that shadow really the Master? Is it the Lord Jesus?"

Overwhelming circumstances are like that storm. Physical and emotional weariness set in, clouding our discernment. Is

---

1. "Be of good cheer" literally translates as "take courage."

Jesus there? Is He speaking? If we can but hear His voice it always brings comfort. "Be of good courage; it is I—the Savior, the Deliverer, the Son of God. Be not afraid."

Peter responded boldly, "Lord, if it be thou, bid me to come unto thee on the water. The voice said, "Come." In all of our struggles, wrestlings, and questions, the only real comfort will be in saying, "Lord, bid me come unto thee!"

Peter walked well for a short time. But the wind and waves were real. Now that he was out of the boat, he was even more vulnerable. Doubt overcame him, and he began to sink. "He cried, saying, Lord, save me. And immediately Jesus stretched forth his hand, and caught him, and said unto him, O thou of little faith, wherefore didst thou doubt? And when they were come into the ship, the wind ceased."

Someday the winds of this life will cease and there will be no more sea to toss our boat. No more wind will howl; no more darkness will blur our vision. If we cast our lives upon Jesus, God Himself will wipe away our tears. Twice Isaiah says, "Therefore the redeemed of the Lord shall return, and come with singing unto Zion; and everlasting joy shall be upon their head: they shall obtain gladness and joy; and sorrow and mourning shall flee away." These are beautiful promises that every one of us should long to secure, especially those who have experienced the pain of tragedy in this fallen world.

"Surely I come quickly. Amen. Even so, come, Lord Jesus. The grace of our Lord Jesus Christ be with you all. Amen."

Bob and Laura Krause
Itasca, Texas
January 2021

Introduction

"The innocence will never last . . ." The song went on, but I do not remember the rest of it. It was a popular tune in the Philippine village where our family lived from 2003 to 2006.

Our son Winston was born September 16, 2005, after five daughters. In our joy after Winston's birth, I had an increasing sense that my life was too good to be real—that somehow, the situation wasn't going to last.

It didn't. In a moment, my innocence was stripped away. Winston died at nine months of age, and our family was thrown into a different life. The old life—the life before part of you dies—was gone. We could never go back.

As Brenda and I searched for meaning and comfort after Winston's death, we were surprised to find that the Bible did not say some of the things we thought it did about death. What God *does say* about death and bad things eventually became our greatest comfort. As you read this book, take time to pray and to meditate on the verses from God's Word.

I wrote this book for those who have faced bad things, but I also wrote it for those who have not. *Your innocence will never last.* Almost certainly, you will experience untimely death, great suffering, rejection, depression, disease, or persecution. There will come times in your life when you will be blinded by tears, searching through the rubble of what you thought was your sturdy house of beliefs.

I thought God answered prayer.
I thought God was here when we needed Him.
I thought God made things work for good.
And on and on.

Nothing I can say in this book will make it easy for you in the day of suffering. No other person will understand exactly what you face. To a greater or lesser degree, you must walk through suffering with God as your only companion, and even God will not always seem to be there for you.

There is an emotional side to suffering. It is deeply personal, full of feeling, besieged by unreconcileable thoughts. Our tendency is to try to find relief from this emotional toll with quick fixes and pat answers. But we must go deep into the Word of God to get the foundation that will carry us through life. Quick fixes and pat answers may soothe our feelings temporarily, but in the end they are merely a manipulation of our minds.

We cannot overcome in suffering by mental power. We cannot "get over" this thing; we cannot go "back to normal." But we can go forward with truth. Truth comes slowly and with difficulty, but as it comes, it works its way into our hearts and becomes a sustaining faith in the Rock of Ages.

If you search for answers in the Rock of Ages, you will find all you need. God may not give all the answers you long for, but He will give you all you *need* to live in hope until the suffering of this life ends.

Though the harsh fact is that innocence can never last, the beautiful truth is that for the child of God, bad things will not last. The wreckage of sin on this earth is overwhelming, but it is temporary. The Bible glows with evidence of a new day just over the horizon. The Son is coming! The eternal God will wipe away all tears.

This book is not an exhaustive work on the ways of God. The ways of God are as much a mystery to me as they are to anyone, and there are depths of that mystery none of us can plumb. Yet God has not surrounded Himself with total mystery. The Bible warmly invites us to seek God and to comprehend what He has told us about Himself. This book discusses some of what God has told us about His ways, and encourages us to align our beliefs with His Word.

More than twenty Christian brothers reviewed this book, criticized it, and suggested improvements. Some of them spent hours in round table discussions considering how to best word these concepts. As a result, nearly every sentence in this book has been agonized over and reworded. I am deeply grateful for the reviewers' help; without them this book would be far less useful. Yet mistakes surely remain, and for them I alone am responsible.

I welcome your conversation on this subject. My contact information is at the beginning of the book.

Michael S. Martin
Mazeppa, Minnesota
December 2020

Part One

Dead Ends

1

Problems, Problems, Problems

Numb with terror, I placed the limp body of my only son on the kitchen table and laid my shaking hands on him.

"Oh God," I cried desperately, "We need a miracle! God, give us a miracle. Heal Winston! We need him, oh God!"

Crying and praying in fear, my wife and daughters stood around us while I frantically gave Winston CPR. But the minutes ticked by, and he did not respond. Finally, we gave up, and only those who have given up can know the impact of those words.

Dreadful, awful, terrible death! Plundering, thieving, pirating death! Cutting, tearing, dividing death! Dark, remorseless, merciless death!

Sometimes we view death as a blessed release, especially when a loved one is suffering pain and disease. Sometimes a sufferer is separated from blissful union with God only by a heart that keeps on beating, beating, beating . . . locking them into a painful earthly existence when all they want to do is be released.

Indeed, release from suffering is a blessing. But the only reason death can be a blessed release is because it frees us from its own effects in our lives. Disease, pain, and sickness are the process of death working on us. We want to die only to escape the effects of death. Were we able to live the beautiful, pain-free, and sin-free life that God intended for mankind, we would never long for death.

Cruel, malicious death! Imprisoning us in a life of hurt and pain; sapping us away as we grow old and feeble; debilitating all of us while occasionally snatching one of us away in the prime of life. One way or another, death teases us, threatens us, buffets us, and finally destroys our physical life. Conniving, contriving death!

But death is not our only problem.

Many grievous things happen in this world, and some of them are worse than death. When once-faithful Christians apostatize, that is worse than death. When our children live in sin, that is worse than death.

More often, the many small problems of daily life perplex our faith. We finally find the car we've been searching for, and a few months later we wreck the vehicle. We finally think we are ready to make some headway on our property debt, and a hospital bill comes. We finally get a superior cow from long and careful breeding, and she breaks her leg.

16

We wake up with a headache, the baby is crying, and we try to make breakfast. As the clock ticks relentlessly on, someone spills the milk, and someone else can't find his clothes. To top it off, the toast burns.

If God loves me, wouldn't He at least make my toaster work? Doesn't He know I was awake half the night with my baby? When everything is going wrong, does He really care? If He really sees every sparrow that falls to the earth, surely He can keep the milk from spilling just this once!

In the next three chapters, we'll explore three common answers to our problems.

2

It's My Fault

Iknow I'm sinful! I haven't been as committed to the Lord as
I should be. I've been coveting a better job. I haven't been
able to pay my debts. I haven't always been kind to my wife.
God is punishing me! I repent!"

Inside the small bamboo house, Juan collapsed weeping
beside the casket of his second infant to die. Most of us wept
with him, but one of his friends had an answer to his heart cry.

"It's always good to repent, Juan," said his friend. "This is an
especially good time, while your heart is softened by losing your
baby. Listen to what God is saying to you. Repent of anything
you know you have done wrong, and the Lord will certainly
bless your life."

Those words helped to confirm two thoughts in Juan's mind. First, his child's death was God's punishment for him as a father. Second, if he had done well, God would have blessed him, and he wouldn't have faced such tragedy. In his tortured mind, there was only conclusion: his child's death was his fault.

Almost everyone who faces the untimely death of someone close to him blames himself for the death. Years ago, one of my friends lost a baby because of congenital problems. Before the child was born, the parents knew it couldn't live. Surely, I supposed, these parents wouldn't blame themselves for their baby's death. The baby hadn't developed a sickness that could have been treated; she hadn't fallen into a tub of water that the parents had left nearby; she hadn't been accidentally run over by a vehicle. What could the parents blame themselves for?

But I was wrong.

"Did I blame myself?" said my friend. "Absolutely. I was the father of my child. She had genetic defects, and they came from me. Every parent of a dead child blames himself for the death. It does not matter whether the death was his fault or not. It is the normal emotional response. It doesn't have to make sense. It is the way we respond, whether it makes sense or not."

One reason we blame ourselves is because there is almost always something we could have done that would have changed the circumstances surrounding the death.

If we hadn't taken that trip when we did, the accident wouldn't have happened. We thought about going a different time, but we didn't do it.

If we hadn't allowed our teenager to drive when we knew he was tired . . .

If we hadn't decided to give the children a ride in the loader bucket . . .

If we hadn't let the children go down the street to play in the park that day . . .

If we hadn't worked on that steep, slippery roof without more safety gear . . .

If we hadn't left Grandpa alone that day . . .

If we had checked Dad's heart condition sooner . . .

One little decision might have altered the course of events. But we didn't make that decision. We might have, but we didn't. Around and around we go.

If only we had thought things through. If only we had done things differently. If only . . .

But we didn't. So it must be our fault.

Is that what God says?

3

It's God's Plan

Michael," the voice on the telephone came distinctly from my friend in America, 10,000 miles away across the Pacific Ocean. "I heard your son died. This is terrible, absolutely terrible."

The voice penetrated my foggy brain. Terrible? Of course.

"I can comfort you with a wonderful thought," my friend went on. "You probably think that it is your fault that Winston died this way."

He paused, and I agreed mentally.

"But it is not your fault," he said confidently. "God did it. Do you know the truth? If Winston had not touched that shorted transformer, he would have fallen down the steps, or been crushed by a vehicle, or simply died for some unexplainable reason. It was just his time to go. God planned that he would live nine months, that's all. You can't go before your time. You can't go after your time. Everyone has his time to go."

Ah, yes. And the Bible says, "My times are in his hand." It's really very simple.

At first thought, this explanation seems to fit when a baby dies of sudden infant death syndrome. It seems to fit, too, when Grandma dies of natural causes after a long, fulfilling life. But how can it fit when angry parents on drugs smother their baby because of his crying? Was *that* God's perfect plan? Was it really their baby's time to go? Would God bring a little innocent soul into the world with the intention of smothering him when he reached a few months of age? Would God create a "perfect plan" of making a couple high on drugs, then causing them to commit murder?

But the questions go deeper yet. If God appoints the hour of your dying, how could you lengthen a society's lifespan by good medical care? How could you improve your health by good eating habits? How could you reduce accidental deaths by additional safety measures? Indeed, how could there be any accidents?

Did God simply decree that people in the Dark Ages would die at about 40 (or much younger), and now decree that many people live past 70?

If God appoints the hour and manner of our dying, did He spread the Black Plague that killed so many people in medieval times?

Did He create Hitler for the purpose of ending millions of precious lives at just the time and manner of God's choosing?

What a revolting thought.

Yet, if we believe that there are no accidents, if we believe that the things we suffer and our deaths are all in the time and manner of God's choosing, then we must believe that.

In the early 1900s, the Primitive Baptists who lived under the high peaks of Virginia's Blue Ridge believed exactly that. In *The Man Who Moved a Mountain*, Bob Childress tells of the ironclad convictions of these mountaineers.

> The big event in the mountains—and one we all went to—was a Primitive Baptist funeral. . . . The more preachers the better. Usually there were four or five who went on all day. Their message seldom varied: God had willed the death, long before the world began.
>
> I'll never forget the first funeral I ever went to. A young man had come home drunk and tried to kill his stepmother, but shot himself instead. I remember yet what one preacher chanted out:
>
> "Little Georgie-a, is a-walkin' the streets of glory-a
> He done exactly what the Lord wanted him to do-a
> When the Lord pulled the foundations of the world-a
> He planned for little Georgie to be born-a
> And to get drunk-a, and to try to shoot his stepmother-a
> And to have the pistol go off and shoot himself-a
> And he fulfilled God's purpose-a
> And he's gone the way God wanted him to go-a
> A man cain't die before his times comes-a, nohow
> Nor in any way nor at any time except as God planned-a
> If he could-a, what would he do when his time comes-a
> Would he die again?"
>
> I suppose I was ten, but I puzzled over that question. . . . When I was eleven I saw something that made me wonder what life was all about. My brothers and I were on our way out hunting when we saw a crowd at Hunter's Chapel, a little church in the woods near us. They were gathered around a gumwood tree. Hanging from a limb was a man with a note pinned to the body: "We kilt him. Hunt us." Many in the crowd were laughing

and smiling. . . . I knew that buried near that very tree there were already thirteen men who had died by guns and knives. Was death any more than a careless mistake, or did God really plan it that way? How could he be a kind God if he burned little girls at the fireplace and made grown men kill and then laugh about it?[1]

Do we serve a God of that character?
Is that what the Bible says?

1. Richard C. Davids, *The Man Who Moved a Mountain* (Philadelphia, Pa.: Fortress Press, 1970), 21-24. Used by permission.

4

It's Fate

No, death isn't your fault. Nor is it God's fault. You do the best you can, and God does the best He can. But there are seven billion people on this planet, and God simply does not reach around.

So goes the reasoning of Rabbi Harold Kuschner, the author of the best-seller *When Bad Things Happen to Good People.*[1]

In other words, fate decides what happens. Fate brings accidents, sickness, and death. Sometimes we can avoid it, and other times there is nothing we can do about it.

My late neighbor Vern Betcher was a prairie farmer near the village of Mazeppa, Minnesota, thirty miles west of the

---

1. (New York, Ny.: Anchor Books, 1981)

Mississippi River. He and his wife Berdeen farmed, trapped, fished, and hunted together. Their life was not easy, but they pulled together, carving their living from the land.

In 1944, Vern and Berdeen had a beautiful baby daughter, Donna Mae. They loved children, and no princess was treated more royally than little Donna Mae.

In the 1940s, wolves and cougars were basically extinct in southeastern Minnesota. But in November and December 1944, another danger prowled the bluffs. Whooping cough struck child after child on scattered farms and in quiet villages. Schools closed, business slowed, and church attendance fell. The dreaded disease closed its tentacles on Vern's home, and little Donna Mae began coughing helplessly. In a few weeks she died, suffocated by mucus and uncontrollable coughing.

Today, my children are growing up less than a mile from where Donna Mae died, and they have little fear of whooping cough. In fact, they are more likely to die of a wolf or cougar attack than of whooping cough.

So did Donna Mae die because of fate? Only because she happened to live near Mazeppa, Minnesota where whooping cough struck in 1944? Only because she happened to be in the age group most susceptible to this disease? Only because she happened to be born before whooping cough vaccine was widespread?

There are some comforting aspects in this theory. If fate carries the blame for bad things, then I am not at fault.

If fate holds the reins of life, if things just happen, it is worthwhile to avoid danger and promote safety and health. Maybe I can prevent something bad from happening, and maybe I can't. But I can try, and part of the time I will win.

If fate is the source of bad things, then God is not the source. He can still be good, kind, and merciful. Even if He can't prevent all suffering, at least He isn't causing suffering.

Another comforting aspect of the fate theory is that there is no evil force bent on making us miserable. There is no hateful being designing bad things for us personally.

But do we really serve a God who is powerful but not all-powerful? One who is present but not present everywhere? One who is very great but just not great enough to get the job done?

Is that what God says?

In the next two chapters, we'll look at the Bible's account of how bad things began.

Part Two

In the Beginning

5

How Evil Came
Into the Universe

Satan's fall and the beginning of evil

Everything that God created was very good. Within that creation there was no sin or badness. Then how did evil begin? Where could bad things come from?

God created heavenly beings—angels, cherubs, heavenly hosts, and sons of God—with the power of choice. One of these beings was Lucifer, the beautiful son of the morning.

But the beautiful son of the morning became the wicked prince of night. Ezekiel 28 and Isaiah 14 describe how this happened. These passages are addressed to the kings of Tyre and Babylon, but the language seems to also refer to Satan, the power behind those heathen kings.

Thou sealest up the sum, full of wisdom, and perfect in beauty. Thou hast been in Eden the garden of God; every precious stone was thy covering. . . . thou wast upon the holy mountain of God; thou hast walked up and down in the midst of the stones of fire.

Thou wast perfect in thy ways from the day that thou wast created, till iniquity was found in thee. . . . thou hast sinned: therefore I will cast thee as profane out of the mountain of God. . . .

Thine heart was lifted up because of thy beauty, thou hast corrupted thy wisdom by reason of thy brightness: I will cast thee to the ground. . . . therefore will I bring forth a fire from the midst of thee, it shall devour thee, and I will bring thee to ashes upon the earth in the sight of all them that behold thee.

All they that know thee among the people shall be astonished at thee: thou shalt be a terror, and never shalt thou be anymore (Ezekiel 28:12-19).

How art thou fallen from heaven, O Lucifer, son of the morning! . . . For thou hast said in thine heart, I will ascend into heaven, I will exalt my throne above the stars of God: I will sit also upon the mount . . . I will ascend above the heights of the clouds; I will be like the most High.

Yet thou shalt be brought down to hell, to the sides of the pit. They that see thee shall narrowly look upon thee, and consider thee, saying, Is this the man that made the earth to tremble, that did shake kingdoms; That made the world as a wilderness, and destroyed the cities thereof; that opened not the house of his prisoners (Isaiah 14:12-17)?

God created Satan perfectly righteous. He loved and served God. However, he could choose to love or hate his Creator, and eventually he chose to hate God.

To be the sum of created wisdom and beauty was not enough for him. To be an anointed cherub in absolute joy was too small for him. He aspired to rule his Creator's universe. He wanted to displace God. He wanted to *be* God.

In that moment, Satan introduced sin to the universe. In that moment, evil first appeared. The first bad thing happened.

God said, "Iniquity was found in thee." God did not make iniquity, He *discovered* iniquity. He first discovered it in Satan.

The devil is a destroyer.

Revelation 9:11 calls the devil the Hebrew name Abaddon and the Greek name Apollyon. Abaddon means "destroying angel" and Apollyon means "destroyer."

The devil can destroy and pervert. He can twist and deform and tangle until God's original creation is all but obliterated, but he cannot create anything from nothing. He is entirely dedicated to ruining what God has made.

Evil came from destruction.

Evil is the result when God's creation is destroyed. When Lucifer's humility was destroyed, he became proud. When his submission was destroyed, he became rebellious. When his holiness was destroyed, he became corrupt. When his truth was destroyed, he became the father of lies.

Satan has no equal to God's rich, satisfying attributes. He only offers absence, vacuum, and emptiness.

That is why "There's nothing out there for a soul that's once known God." That is the terror of sin. No peace, no satisfaction, no joy, and in the end, no communication with God.

Evil is weaker than good.

Good and evil are not equal powers. We tend to think of evil as the equal of good—or even stronger than good—because many people turn from light and walk in darkness. We see sin grow while righteousness seems to wane. Truth seems to lie dead in the streets while deception flourishes. But this is temporary. In the end, God will reward all righteousness and judge all sin.

We know good is stronger than evil because we can choose eternal salvation. If Satan was stronger than God, he would force us to suffer forever. If Satan was stronger than God, he would not allow any possibility but total ruin for mankind.

In no way is evil the equal of good. Humility is stronger than pride. Submission is stronger than rebellion. Holiness is stronger than corruption. Truth is stronger than lies. Heaven is greater than hell. God is much more powerful than the devil![1]

Evil is real even though it was not created.

Blindness is real, but it was not created. Blindness only exists because of sight; blindness is the lack of sight. Rot is real, but it only exists in something that was once sound; it is the lack of soundness. So evil is not something that God made; it is the real lack of the things that God made.

Evil is a real lack of good.

A "real lack" of good means more than just the absence of good. A tree cannot see, but that is no lack; it was not made to see. But if you cannot see, you have a real lack. Something is wrong.

When people disobey God, they have a real lack. They are not whole. They cannot be what they were meant to be.

However, I do not say that evil is *merely* the lack of good. Evil is not *mere*. It is a deadly, observable rebellion. It is real, horrifying, and powerful.

Evil is not eternal.

Sin and corruption are not eternal; they began in Satan. Holiness and purity are eternal absolutes; but sin and

---
1. Revelation 20:1-3

corruption are not absolutes. They are rebellion against eternal absolutes.

Good and evil are presently locked in a struggle, but they are not locked in an *eternal* struggle. In eternity past, God lived alone; there was no evil. In eternity future, God will "sever the wicked from among the just."[2] There is a "great gulf" between good and evil.[3] Already the devil is chained, and he will eventually be cast into the lake of fire along with his followers.[4]

Righteousness does not require evil.

God was true before falsehood existed. God loved before there was hate. God was light before there was spiritual darkness. Purity existed before there was lust. Truth, love, light, and purity existed without their opposites.

Therefore, righteousness, love, light, and God's other attributes are the original qualities. Evil is the impostor.

However, evil requires righteousness.

Unholiness could not exist without holiness. Impurity could not exist without purity. Death could not exist without life. Lies, hate, spiritual darkness, and lust could not exist without their opposites.

Therefore, God's attributes are the original qualities. Sin and death are the result of rebelling against God's original qualities.

The devil is the original rebel, and in him was the original lack of all good things. So, in him was the original existence of bad things. That is why bad things exist without God having made them.

---

2. Matthew 13:49
3. Luke 16:26
4. Revelation 20

Study Questions

1. Satan was once a perfectly righteous, holy angel. Why is understanding this so important?

2. For what reason(s) did Satan fall?

3. How are we tempted to think as Satan did?

4. "In no way is evil the equal of good." Then why do so many people choose evil?

5. List some Bible concepts that keep us anchored in the truth that good is greater than evil.

6

How Evil Came
Into the World

"By one man sin entered into the world"

S atan's fall created a spiritual realm of evil. However, it did not automatically bring evil to mankind and the earth. Satan could tempt man, but he could not introduce evil into the world unless man chose to obey him.

Adam and Eve's spirits were holy, their minds were righteous, and their world was flawless. They were innocent.

Though Adam was innocent, he knew something of what "evil" and "die" meant. God said to him, "Of every tree of the garden thou mayest freely eat: But of the tree of the knowledge of good and evil, thou shalt not eat of it: for in the day that thou eatest thereof thou shalt surely die."

How mankind fell

If man had obeyed God, evil would have remained in the fallen spiritual realm. Mankind would have remained practically ignorant of the rebellion in the spiritual world.

But that is not what happened.

> Now the serpent was more subtil than any beast of the field which the LORD God had made. And he said unto the woman, Yea, hath God said, Ye shall not eat of every tree of the garden?
>
> And the woman said unto the serpent, We may eat of the fruit of the trees of the garden: But of the fruit of the tree which is in the midst of the garden, God hath said, Ye shall not eat of it, neither shall ye touch it, lest ye die.
>
> And the serpent said unto the woman, Ye shall not surely die: For God doth know that in the day ye eat thereof, then your eyes shall be opened, and ye shall be as gods, knowing good and evil.
>
> And when the woman saw that the tree was good for food, and that it was pleasant to the eyes, and a tree to be desired to make one wise, she took of the fruit thereof, and did eat, and gave also unto her husband with her; and he did eat.
>
> And the eyes of them both were opened, and they knew that they were naked; and they sewed fig leaves together, and made themselves aprons (Genesis 3:1-7).

The Fall's effect on people

Their eyes opened; they knew evil (Genesis 3:7, 22). Knowing evil brought the fallen nature and inclination to be evil.[1]

They lived in guilt, fear, and blame (3:8-13). The Fall brought the shame of nakedness. Adam and Eve had lost the robe of innocence, and they hid from God. When God found them, Adam blamed Eve and Eve blamed the serpent, but God blamed all three.

---

1. Romans 7:14

Man entered a state of enmity with the devil (3:15). Since the Fall, the devil has tempted, trapped, and tortured man.

Woman now faces sorrow, pain, and unkind domination (3:16). Since the Fall, childbearing causes woman much pain.

Woman was to assist man as he led the human home. But since the Fall, she suffers greatly from the thoughtless and unkind leadership of carnal man.

Woman was to be cared for and sheltered by man. But now she suffers untold sorrow from the lusts of godless man.

Man now faces sorrow, struggle, and ceaseless toil to provide a living for his family (3:17-19). Before the Fall, man kept Eden, a pleasant and rewarding task. But since the Fall, man must keep the fallen, groaning earth. He must sweat and toil.

Man had to leave God's garden (3:22-24). Man had chosen to obey the devil instead of God, so he no longer had a place in Eden. In that way, eviction from Eden was judgment. But eviction from Eden was also a mercy. The tree of life was in Eden, and if man had eaten of it, he would have lived forever in his sad, fallen state.

Man will die (3:19). Man walked out of God's rule (life) into the devil's domination (death). Therefore, man is to blame for the presence of sin and death in the world. "Wherefore, as by one man sin entered into the world, and death by sin; and so death passed upon all men, for that all have sinned" (Romans 5:12).

Is it fair that we suffer just because Adam and Eve fell?

Why don't you and I have the same opportunity Adam and Eve did? God gave them a pristine, holy world, but we are born into a fallen world saturated with sin.

First, we do not suffer just because Adam and Eve fell. As Merle Ruth says,

> God allows suffering because it is part of the package that man chose and continues to choose. Prior to the Fall, man was warned that disobedience would yield grave consequences. . . . So then, after the first pair had sinned, God immediately informed them that a new dimension would enter their lives—hardship, sorrow, and suffering. God has never rescinded that sentence. Neither have men stopped making the choice initially made by Adam and Eve.[2]

Like Adam and Eve, you and I also chose, at one point or another, to sin. So, we suffer for our own sinful choices, not merely for Adam and Eve's choice.

However, we can still ask: Is it fair that you and I do not have the same circumstances that Adam and Eve had in Eden? You and I chose sin, to be sure, but death had already come into the world. Our environment is full of sin, so we really do not have the same opportunity as Adam and Eve.

Certainly, Adam and Eve had circumstances that have never been repeated. In that way, they had an advantage over us. But consider our advantage over them. We live in a time when we can choose Jesus Christ, and He will cleanse us from sin. Further, He sends us His Holy Spirit and gives us the power to live in victory. He also promises that we can live with Him eternally in the new heaven and earth, a place that exceeds the joy of Eden without the possibility of sin!

Instead of asking why we can't go back to Eden (where we may have made the same choice as Adam and Eve), I ask: Do we deserve salvation? Do we deserve the sufferings of Jesus Christ for us? Do we deserve eternal life? Do we deserve a

---

2. *Triumphant in Suffering* (Crockett, Ky.: Rod and Staff Publishers, 1991) p. 14.

personal relationship with "the Father of mercies, and the God of all comfort"? These are God's gifts to undeserving people who repent.

Who wants to go back to Eden when we can go forward to eternity with Christ?

Study Questions

1. "And the LORD God said, Behold, the man is become as one of us, to know good and evil" (Genesis 3:22). How did man's knowledge of good and evil change in the Fall?

2. List some historical consequences of the Fall and their counterparts in our world.

3. Explain the last sentence in the quote in the last section. "Neither have men stopped making the choice initially made by Adam and Eve."

4. Why is it right to praise God for His gifts to us instead of blaming Him for not giving us the opportunity that Adam and Eve had?

Part Three

Life In a Fallen World

7

"I Wondered if the Lord Had Planned for Me to Kill a Man"

Does God cause people to sin?

In Chapter 3 I introduced Bob Childress, a ten-year-old boy in the mountains of West Virginia who puzzled over the teaching that God planned everything. When Bob was fifteen, he was still mulling over such questions.

> Once I was watching a poker game when two good friends started arguing over a two-cent stake. In a flash, one shot the other dead. At the funeral, the preacher said, "This is a fearsome thing, but since it be the Lord's will, it had to be. Man ain't got nothing to do with it. He dies when his time comes, and he cain't die before." I didn't know what to believe. I wondered if the Lord had planned for me to kill a man—or to be killed."[1]

---

1. *The Man Who Moved a Mountain*, ibid., 26, 27.

The question that confused Bob Childress in 1905 is still confusing many Christians today. Think about the statements that people commonly make about things that happen.

"It was supposed to be, or it wouldn't have happened."

"Everything that happens is in God's plan."

"God has a reason for everything."

These statements imply that only God is at work in the world. But the Bible teaches that Satan is also working here, and that the world is a battleground between God and Satan.

Perhaps you are thinking that these statements simply convey trust in a sovereign God. But do they? Let's examine some ways in which these statements are inconsistent with the Bible's message.

If we believe that everything that happens is "supposed to be," we must believe that God causes us to fall into sin.

There could be no greater impediment to the fight of faith than the belief that our Captain occasionally forces us to lose a battle, yet that is exactly what many theologians teach. Consider this example from *Suffering and the Sovereignty of God*.

> God's foreordination is the ultimate reason why everything comes about, including the existence of all evil persons and things and the occurrence of any evil acts or events. And so [God is] the creator, sender, the permitter, and sometimes even the instigator of evil.[2]

If God plans and causes everything that happens, then He caused Satan to fall. If He did so, Satan did not disobey God; he did God's will. Then why has God reserved him for eternal punishment?

---

2. From *Suffering and the Sovereignty of God*, John Piper and Justin Taylor, et. al., 2006, pp. 43, 44. Used by permission of Crossway, a publishing ministry of Good News Publishers, Wheaton, Il., 60187. (www.crossway. org).

If God causes everything, He causes us to sin. If it is His will for us to sin, why does He tell us not to sin?

If sin comes from God, why does the Bible insist that sin entered the world by the devil through man's fall? If God plans and causes sin, why does He claim to be holy and to hate sin?

Why does God pronounce woe on people who "call evil good, and good evil"[3] if He is creating and doing both?

A house divided against itself cannot stand.

In Matthew 12, Jesus healed a devil-possessed person. "This fellow doth not cast out devils," the Pharisees mocked, "but by Beelzebub the prince of the devils."

> And Jesus knew their thoughts, and said unto them, Every kingdom divided against itself is brought to desolation; and every city or house divided against itself cannot stand: And if Satan cast out Satan, he is divided against himself; how shall then his kingdom stand? . . .
>
> Or else how can one enter into a strong man's house, and spoil his goods, except he first bind the strong man? and then he will spoil his house (Matthew 12:25, 26, 29).

No kingdom that fights itself survives. God commands us to be holy, and He does not contradict Himself by causing us to sin. God commands us to "hate the evil, and love the good"[4] because there *is* good and evil! He is for the good, and against the evil, and He calls us to the same position.

God is light; Satan is darkness. Light and darkness cannot mix. God is always holy and good. Since his fall, Satan is always corrupt and evil.

Therefore, the evil that we see in the world or in our own lives is not from God. The Biblical conclusion is that God *does*

3. Isaiah 5:20
4. Amos 5:15

not plan, cause, and purpose everything that happens in the universe or in our lives.

Read the following story, asking yourself this question: Does the sovereignty of God mean that He was causing Madalyn to do all she did?

"My mother was indeed an evil person."

On June 17, 1963, the Supreme Court of the United States announced their decision that Bible reading and prayer in public schools was unconstitutional. One of the influential people in that case was Madalyn Murray O'Hair, a divorced woman from Baltimore. Her son William said that she was controlled by demons. However, if God causes all that happens in the world, then God caused Madalyn to live as she did.

Madalyn was born in 1919, the second child of a young couple that did not want her. In 1941, she married an Ohio native named John Roths. Two months later, after the Japanese bombed Pearl Harbor, Madalyn and John both went to war. She went to Europe, and he to the Pacific.

In the army, Madalyn worked closely with high-ranking officials. When the war was over, she was with child by an officer named William Murray Jr., a married Catholic. Madalyn wanted Murray to leave his wife and marry her. He would not, he said, because of his Catholic principles.

Disgusted and frustrated, Madalyn returned home. She found her parents living in Ohio in a shack with a dirt floor, without electricity or running water. Her father had spent every penny she sent home from the war, mostly on alcohol. Angered by her poverty and her parents, bitter at Mr. Murray and the

Catholic religion, Madalyn became increasingly antagonistic toward God.

During a thunderstorm one summer evening before her baby was born, Madalyn suddenly announced, "I'm going out in that storm to challenge God to strike me and this child dead by lightning. Come and watch!"

As her mother and brother watched, she strode dramatically out into the storm, shook her hand menacingly at the heavens, and shouted blasphemies. After waiting for a while, she returned triumphantly to the house, declaring that God could not exist. "If God exists, He would surely have taken up my challenge. I've proved irrefutably that God does not exist!"

Nearly every day, Madalyn argued ferociously with her father and screamed obscenities at him. She claimed to hate America and was fascinated with socialism and Communism. She was never able to keep a job for long. Her relationships were so dysfunctional that her son William did not even know that she was his mother until he was eight years old.

In 1960, Madalyn turned her guns on school prayer and Bible reading, eventually culminating in the fateful 1963 Supreme Court decision. Meanwhile, in 1962, she became editor of the *American Atheist* magazine. Several times in this period she tried to murder her father. She publicly described herself as an offensive, unlovable, bull-headed, defiant, and aggressive slob.

When the public school prayer case was over, Madalyn sued the city of Baltimore to prevent them from exempting churches from taxes. One person who interviewed "Mad Murray," as Madalyn began to call herself, wrote of her as a "strange, immensely complicated woman, full of paradoxes, conflicts, and challenges." She would "say anything, do anything, believe anything as long as it was rebellious and antisocial." She wanted to be able to walk down any street in America and not see a sign of Christianity. "I love a good fight," she said. "I guess fighting God and God's spokesmen is sort of the ultimate, isn't it?"

In Madalyn's atheist organization, she surrounded herself with dangerous male criminals and tried to control them. In 1995, one of them brutally murdered her.

Her son William had become a Christian in 1980. In his book *My Life Without God,*[5] he said that his mother delighted in depravity. She was evil, he wrote, not necessarily because of her role in removing prayer from America's schools, but because her whole life focused on immorality. She stole large amounts of money, abused people's trust, swindled children out of their inheritances, cheated on her taxes, and even stole from her own organizations.

Now, how have you answered the question I asked at the beginning of this story? *Does the sovereignty of God mean that He caused Madalyn to do what she did?* The answer cannot be yes, because the New Testament shows us that Madalyn was living in defiant rebellion against God's will.

The Biblical conclusion is that God *did not* plan and cause everything that Madalyn experienced and did. Nor does He plan and cause the sin that you and I commit.

Certainly God received glory from Madalyn's life, though it was in the fact that her efforts to dethrone Him could not reduce Him one iota. "Surely the wrath of man shall praise thee," says Psalm 76:10. But the fact that God is praised even by man's wrath does not make Him the Creator of their wrath!

---

5. William J. Murray, (Washington, D.C.: WND Books, 2012), 311.

The source of sin

Listen to the apostle James explaining the source of sin.

> Blessed is the man that endureth temptation . . . Let no man say when he is tempted, I am tempted of God: for God cannot be tempted with evil, neither tempteth he any man: But every man is tempted, when he is drawn away of his own lust, and enticed. Then when lust hath conceived, it bringeth forth sin: and sin, when it is finished, bringeth forth death.
>
> Do not err, my beloved brethren. Every good gift and every perfect gift is from above, and cometh down from the Father of lights, with whom is no variableness, neither shadow of turning (James 1:12-17).

Do not err, my beloved brethren! Sin and its darkness does not come from the Father of lights. But James isn't finished.

> From whence come wars and fightings among you? come they not hence, even of your lusts that war in your members? Ye lust, and have not: ye kill, and desire to have, and cannot obtain: ye fight and war . . . . Ye adulterers and adulteresses, know ye not that the friendship of the world is enmity with God? whosoever therefore will be a friend of the world is the enemy of God. . . . God resisteth the proud, but giveth grace unto the humble. Submit yourselves therefore to God. Resist the devil, and he will flee from you (James 4:1-7).

Sin comes from our lusts, not from God. Sin and lust are results of the devil's work. Sin and lust make us enemies of God.

God works in the world, and the devil fights Him. You and I must choose which of these masters we will follow.[6]

My sin, my sin, my sin

In Psalm 51, King David's prayer of repentance after he had sinned with Bathsheba, David acknowledges seven times that his sin was *his own sin*. David realizes in verse 5 that he

---

6. Matthew 6:24

was plagued from birth by the sin nature, yet he did not blame Adam for his personal fall into sin.

David acknowledges throughout the Psalms that "the steps of a good man are ordered by the Lord," but he does not blame God for guiding his steps into adultery. Instead, David states that his sin was evil and against God's will, and that God was just to judge him for this sin.

Our sin is not God's sin. It is not Adam's sin. It is *our* sin. "But *your* iniquities have separated between you and your God, and *your* sins have hid his face from you."[7]

God would not convict us for sin if He caused us to sin. God is just when He holds us responsible for our sin.

But Ephesians 1:11 states that Jesus Christ "worketh all things after the counsel of His own will." Doesn't that include the sin in our lives?

Doesn't "all things" mean everything that exists? "Worketh" does not mean *permits* or *allows*, it means that Christ is actively *doing* "all things" after the counsel of His will.

Imagine that you are a house builder. Today you had a customer who was anxious to have his house roofed before a rain, but two of your employees called in sick. The supply company did not deliver the roofing material until noon, and when you finally started the job, your lift broke down. The local parts store did not have the lift part you needed; the company will ship it and it will arrive in two days.

At the end of the day, you told someone that it seemed like everything was against you today. Did you mean that God, your family, and your friends were against you? Did you

---

7. Isaiah 59:2, emphasis added.

mean that your church was against you? Did you mean that the government of your country and the United Nations was against you?

Of course not. You meant what you were talking about, and everyone understands that. Just so, Ephesians 1:11 must be understood in its context. The focus of Ephesians 1 is how God made us His children by redemption through Christ's blood.

Ephesians 1:11 simply means that Jesus Christ is working *all things about our salvation* after the counsel of His own will. According to Ephesians 1, nothing can alter or destroy God's plan to redeem people who trust in Him.

Ephesians 1:11 does not mean that God caused Mao Tsetung and Adolf Hitler to kill and persecute millions of people. Nor does it mean that Jesus Christ eternally planned for you to have toast and cereal for breakfast this morning, or that the fly that just flew past you and buzzed on the window did so because He eternally planned for that fly to do that maneuver in this instant. Ephesians 1:11 is not a rationale for murders, heart attacks, and auto accidents.

"Worketh all things after the counsel of His own will" cannot mean that everything that happens is God's will, for 2 Timothy 2:26 states that the devil is taking some people captive "at his will." Some things happen by the devil's will, not God's will.

But didn't God cause Judas to sin?

Acts 1:16 says "this scripture must needs have been fulfilled, which the Holy Ghost by the mouth of David spake before concerning Judas." Many theologians teach that prophecy destined Judas to fall.[8]

---

8. See Psalm 41:9. This Scripture, along with Psalm 109:8, 9 appears to be the prophecies to which Acts 1:16 refers.

John 6:64 states that Jesus "knew from the beginning" who would betray Him. But foreknowledge is not foreordination. God did not cause Judas be the betrayer. The Old Testament prophesied that someone would betray Jesus, but Judas did not have to be that betrayer. The New Testament says that Judas fulfilled Scripture, not that Judas had to fulfill Scripture.

Judas "had obtained part of this ministry." But he lost that apostleship "by transgression." Instead of going where God wanted him to go, he chose to go to "his own place."[9]

Luke 22 and John 13 say that Satan entered into Judas. Before Judas left the Last Supper, intending to betray Jesus, Jesus did not say to him, "Do quickly what I am making you do." No, He said, "That *thou* doest, do quickly." Judas became "the son of perdition"[10] by his own choice, not by God's choice.

Did God cause King David to sin in numbering Israel's soldiers?

> And again the anger of the Lord was kindled against Israel, and he moved David against them to say, Go, number Israel and Judah. . . .
>
> And Joab said unto the king, Now the Lord thy God add unto the people, how many soever they be, an hundredfold, that the eyes of my lord the king may see it: but why doth my lord the king delight in this thing? Notwithstanding the king's word prevailed against Joab. . . .
>
> And David's heart smote him after that he had numbered the people. And David said unto the Lord, I have sinned greatly in that I have done: and now, I beseech thee, O Lord, take away the iniquity of thy servant; for I have done very foolishly (2 Samuel 24:1, 3, 4, 10)

9. Acts 1:17-25
10. John 17:12

In a review of the same incident, 1 Chronicles 21:1 states that "Satan stood up against Israel, and provoked David to number Israel."

It is obvious in this story that God did not make David sin; David *had already sinned* with vain ambition. Nor did God make Israel sin. They had already sinned, therefore He was angry with them. God's work was to bring this sinning king and nation to the point where He could show them the seriousness of their error and recover them for Himself. But the wrong attitudes and the sin were theirs, not God's.

God allowed Satan to provoke David, but He chastened Israel through the unavoidable consequences of this sin. Satan wanted to take Israel away from God, but in the end, Israel repented and renewed their spiritual life. Satan's design failed.

Does God simply plan and cause sin without becoming sinful?

Many people claim that He does. They point out that "God moves in a mysterious way," and Isaiah 55:8, 9 says:

> For my thoughts are not your thoughts, neither are your ways my ways, saith the Lord.
> For as the heavens are higher than the earth, so are my ways higher than your ways, and my thoughts than your thoughts.

Far from saying that God in His mystery causes sin, these verses are a warm invitation to mankind, "Come! Follow My ways, and think My thoughts!" Verses 7-9 emphasize that we do not think as God wants us to. God wants us to forsake our unrighteous thoughts, and think His thoughts.

Certainly, God's judgments are unsearchable, and His ways are past finding out.[11] But He is not the cause of sin, mysteriously or otherwise.

We can know good and evil at sight.

One of the great principles of the New Testament is that we can know good and evil at sight. We can know when we are seeing God's work and when we are seeing Satan's work.

> Ye shall know them by their fruits. Do men gather grapes of thorns, or figs of thistles? Even so every good tree bringeth forth good fruit; but a corrupt tree bringeth forth evil fruit.
>
> A good tree cannot bring forth evil fruit, neither can a corrupt tree bring forth good fruit (Matthew 7:16-18).

God wills good fruit. In the end, He will not tell sinners, "I planned and caused your sin." Instead, He will tell them, "I never knew you." Their evil is not from Him.

God does not cause us to sin. We do not need to wonder whether God has planned that we will kill a man. He has not, and He will not.

Study Questions

1. Why is it inconsistent with the Bible message to claim that Satan follows God's will?

2. Give Biblical evidence that God does not plan or cause the sins we commit.

3. Since the ultimate source of sin is Satan, why does God hold us responsible for our sin?

11. Romans 11:33

4. Using Bible examples, explain how important it is to understand Scripture passages in their context.

5. Why is the principle of knowing good and evil "by their fruits" so important?

8

"Never Shall I Forget Those Flames That Consumed My Faith Forever"

Does God cause atrocity?

Elie Wiesel was only twelve years old, but already he was a deeply observant Jew. By day, he studied the Talmud. Each evening, he went to the synagogue to weep and pray over the destruction of the Temple. He longed to ask God the questions that plagued him, and to understand God's replies.

All that was before Hitler's troops had penetrated to Sighet, Wiesel's small hometown in Hungary. Before sealed cattle cars, crammed with human cargo, bore Elie Wiesel and his fellow

Jews to concentration camps. Before the doors slid open, and the cargo numbly walked through aisles of men with machine guns.

"Men to the left. Women to the right!" Eight words spoken quietly, indifferently, without emotion. Eight simple, short words. Yet that was the moment when I left my mother. There was no time to think, and I already felt my father's hand press against mine: we were alone. In a fraction of a second I could see my mother, my sisters, move to the right. Tzipora was holding Mother's hand. I saw them walking farther and farther away: Mother was stroking my sister's blond hair, as if to protect her. And I walked on with my father, with the men. I didn't know that this was the moment in time and place where I was leaving my mother and Tzipora forever. . . .

"Poor devils, you are heading for the crematorium." He seemed to be telling the truth. Not far from us, flames, huge flames, were rising from a ditch. Something was being burned there. A truck drew close and unloaded its hold: small children. . . . So that was where we were going. A little farther on, there was another, larger pit for adults.

I pinched myself: Was I still alive? Was I awake? How was it possible that men, women, and children were being burned and the world kept silent? No. All this could not be real. A nightmare perhaps . . . Soon I would wake up with a start, my heart pounding, and find that I was back in the room of my childhood, with my books . . .

My father's voice tore me from my daydreams:

"What a shame, a shame that you did not go with your mother . . . I saw many children your age go with their mothers . . ."

His voice was terribly sad. I understood that he did not wish to see what they would do to me. He did not wish to see his only son go up in flames.

My forehead was covered with cold sweat. Still, I told him that I could not believe that human beings were being burned in our times; the world would never tolerate such crimes . . .

"The world? The world is not interested in us. Today, everything is possible, even the crematoria . . ." His voice broke.

"Father," I said. "If that is true, then I don't want to wait. I'll run into the electrified barbed wire. That would be easier than a slow death in the flames."

He didn't answer. He was weeping. His body was shaking. Everybody around us was weeping. . . .

"*Yisgadal, veyiskadash, shmey raba* . . . May His name be celebrated and sanctified . . ." whispered my father.

For the first time, I felt anger rising within me. Why should I sanctify His name? The Almighty, the eternal and terrible Master of the Universe, chose to be silent. What was there to thank Him for?

We continued our march. We were coming closer and closer to the pit, from which an infernal heat was rising. Twenty more steps. If I was going to kill myself, this was the time. Our column had only fifteen steps to go. I bit my lips so that my father would not hear my teeth chattering. Ten more steps. Eight. Seven. We were walking slowly, as one follows a hearse, our own funeral procession. Only four more steps. Three. There it was now, very close to us, the pit and its flames. I gathered all that remained of my strength in order to break rank and throw myself onto the barbed wire. Deep down, I was saying good-bye to my father, to the whole universe, and, against my will, I found myself whispering the words: "*Yisgadal, veyiskadash, shmey raba* . . . May His name be exalted and sanctified . . . " My heart was about to burst. There. I was face-to-face with the Angel of Death . . .

No. Two steps from the pit, we were ordered to turn left and herded into barracks. . . .

Never shall I forget that night, the first night in camp, that turned my life into one long night seven times sealed.

Never shall I forget that smoke.

Never shall I forget the small faces of the children whose bodies I saw transformed into smoke under a silent sky.

Never shall I forget those flames that consumed my faith forever.

Never shall I forget the nocturnal silence that deprived me for all eternity of the desire to live.

Never shall I forget those moments that murdered my God and my soul and turned my dreams to ashes.

Never shall I forget those things, even were I condemned to live as long as God himself.

Never.

The barrack we had been assigned to was very long. On the roof, a few bluish skylights. I thought: This is what the antechamber of hell must look like. So many crazed men, so much shouting, so much brutality.

With thousands of other inmates, Elie was forced to watch senseless hangings. Once, two men and a young boy were condemned to death. The boy was delicate and beautiful, and everyone in the camp loved him. His face, Elie wrote, was the face of an angel in distress.

The SS seemed more preoccupied, more worried, than usual. To hang a child in front of thousands of onlookers was not a small matter. The head of the camp read the verdict. All eyes were on the child. He was pale, almost calm, but he was biting his lips as he stood in the shadow of the gallows. . . .

The three condemned prisoners stepped together onto the chairs. In unison, the nooses were placed around their necks.

"Long live liberty!" shouted the two men.

But the boy was silent.

"Where is merciful God, where is He?" someone behind me was asking.

At the signal, the three chairs were tipped over.

Total silence in the camp. On the horizon, the sun was setting.

"Caps off!" screamed the *Lageralteste*. His voice quivered. As for the rest of us, we were weeping.

"Cover your heads!"

Then came the march past the victims. . . . Behind me, I heard the same man asking:

"For God's sake, where is God?"

And from within me, I heard a voice answer:

"Where He is? This is where—hanging here from this gallows . . ."

On the eve of Rosh Hashanah,[1] the last day of that cursed
year, the entire camp was agitated and every one of us felt the
tension. . . .

The evening meal was distributed, an especially thick
soup, but nobody touched it. We wanted to wait until after
prayer. On the *Appelplatz*, surrounded by electrified barbed
wire, thousands of Jews, anguish on their faces, gathered in
silence. . . .

What are You, my God? I thought angrily. How do You
compare to this stricken mass gathered to affirm to you their
faith, their anger, their defiance? What does your grandeur
mean, Master of the Universe, in the face of all this cowardice,
this decay, this misery? Why do you go on troubling these poor
people's wounded minds, their ailing bodies? . . .

"Blessed be the Almighty . . ."

The voice of the officiating inmate had just become audible.
At first I thought it was the wind.

"Blessed be God's name . . ."

Thousands of lips repeated the benediction, bent over like
trees in a storm.

Blessed be God's name?

Why, but why would I bless Him? Every fiber in me
rebelled. Because He caused thousands of children to burn in
His mass graves? Because He kept six crematoria working day
and night, including Sabbath and the Holy Days? Because in
His great might, He had created Auschwitz, Birkenau, Buna,
and so many other factories of death? How could I say to Him:
Blessed be Thou, Almighty, Master of the Universe, who chose
us among all nations to be tortured day and night, to watch as
our fathers, our mothers, our brothers end up in the furnaces?

---

1. Rosh Hashanah is the Jewish New Year, a solemn occasion celebrated by many
Jews.

Praised be The Holy Name, for having chosen us to be slaughtered on Thine altar?

I listened as the inmate's voice rose; it was powerful yet broken, amid the weeping, the sobbing, the sighing of the entire "congregation":

"All the earth and universe are God's!" . . .

And I, the former mystic, was thinking: Yes, man is stronger, greater than God. When Adam and Eve deceived You, You chased them from paradise. When You were displeased by Noah's generation, You brought down the Flood. When Sodom lost Your favor, You caused the heavens to rain down fire and damnation. But look at these men whom You have betrayed, allowing them to be tortured, slaughtered, gassed, and burned, what do they do? They pray before You! They praise Your name!

"All of creation bears witness to the Greatness of God!"

In days gone by, Rosh Hashanah had dominated my life. I knew that my sins grieved the Almighty and so I pleaded for forgiveness. . . .

But now, I no longer pleaded for anything. I was no longer able to lament. On the contrary, I felt very strong. I was the accuser, God the accused. My eyes had opened and I was alone, terribly alone in a world without God, without man. Without love or mercy. I was nothing but ashes now, but I felt myself to be stronger than this Almighty to whom my life had been bound for so long. . . .

I knew a rabbi, from a small town in Poland. He was old and bent, his lips constantly trembling. He was always praying, in the block, at work, in the ranks. He recited entire pages from the Talmud, arguing with himself, asking and answering himself endless questions. One day, he said to me:

"It's over. God is no longer with us."

And as though he regretted having uttered such words so coldly, so dryly, he added in his broken voice, "I know. No one has the right to say things like that. I know that very well. Man is too insignificant, too limited, to even try to comprehend

God's mysterious ways. But what can someone like myself do? I'm neither a sage nor a just man. I am not a saint. I'm a simple creature of flesh and bone. I suffer hell in my soul and my flesh. I also have eyes and I see what is being done here. Where is God's mercy? Where's God? How can I believe, how can anyone believe in this God of Mercy?"[2]

There are no words for this terror. Anyone who suffers like this possesses a sort of authority—how can we question their conclusions? But does the Bible agree with these conclusions?

If God ordains everything that happens, He planned and caused the Holocaust.

Was Elie right when he said that God caused thousands of children to burn, that God kept six crematoria working day and night, and that He created death factories? Was he correct when he concluded that God chose the Jews to be tortured and to watch their loved ones fed to furnaces?

Some Christian theologians say he was right. In *Suffering and the Sovereignty of God*, John Piper insists that God Himself causes all evil for His own glory.

> This includes—as incredible and as unacceptable as it may currently seem—God's even having brought about the Nazis' brutality at Birkenau and Auschwitz as well as the terrible killings of Dennis Rader and even the sexual abuse of a young child . . . . Nothing that exists or occurs falls outside of God's ordaining will.
>
> Nothing, including no evil person or thing or event or deed. [3]

---

2. Excerpts from *Night* by Elie Wiesel, translated by Marion Wiesel. Translation copyright 2006 by Marion Wiesel, pp. 29, 32, 33, 34, 64-68, 76, 77. Reprinted by permission of Hill and Wang, a division of Farrar, Straus, and Giroux. All rights reserved.
3. *Suffering and the Sovereignty of God*, ibid., 42, 43. Used by permission.

Adolf Hitler himself inferred that God was sustaining the German cause: "If the [Germans] despair, I will not be sorry for them if God lets them down."[4]

In the end, Elie Wiesel lost his faith. Nor did he accept the Christian faith. And I can understand why, if all Elie knew of Christians was that they, too, believed that God caused the Nazis' brutality. Long before the Nazis, Germany was infected with the doctrine that everything that happens is God's will.

If God did all things recorded in human history, His nature is terribly unjust and contradictory. Jesus Christ said that one who offends a child would be punished with everlasting fire.[5] Is it possible that God the Father, who is one with His Son Jesus Christ, willed thousands of innocent little children to be thrown to the flames under the silent German sky?

If God caused all those things, why does His anger burn against the people who did them? Why would He deliver them into hell if they performed His will? Why does His image within us cry out that these things are terribly unrighteous?

According to one Holocaust survivor, there are basically two responses to this terrifying suffering.[6]

> They are, either complete submission to God, capitulation to His enormous incomprehensible inscrutable will; or blaspheming Him, cursing Him, not really denying Him but detesting Him, despising Him, menacing Him; threatening Him, threatening to withhold faith in Him: "God, if you don't do something I'm going to stop believing in you . . ."

---

4. Speech at Munich, broadcast on November 8, 1943.
5. Matthew 18:1-10.
6. The Holocaust survivor quotes are copyright 1980 from *The Faith and Doubt of Holocaust Survivors* by Reeve Robert Brenner (New York: The Free Press), pp. 100, 102, 103. Reproduced by permission of Taylor and Francis Group, LLC, a division of Informa plc.

But are those the only possible conclusions? Do we have to accept everything as God's "enormous incomprehensible inscrutable will," or lose our sanity and blaspheme and curse Him? The Bible indicates otherwise, and so do some other Holocaust survivors. One of them testified as follows.

> The camps had nothing to do with God; and God, while not "on vacation" or absent from them, cannot be blamed for them. . . . It just never occurred to me to associate the calamity we were experiencing with God, to blame Him, or to believe in Him less or to cease believing in Him at all because He didn't come to our aid.
>
> God doesn't owe us that. . . . If someone believes God is responsible for the death of six million because He didn't somehow do something to save them, he's got his thinking reversed. We owe God our lives for the few or many years we live, and we have the duty to worship Him and do all that He commands us. That's what we're here on this earth for, to be in God's service, to do God's bidding, to be God's people . . . Sometimes it means suffering, but it's not because God wants us to suffer. It's because other people hate us.

Another survivor had similar sentiments.

> Confined within the barbed wire of Auschwitz I understood to separate the wicked deeds of men from the workings of the entire universe. The system of the world and the idea behind its functioning is God. I have always believed that. . . .
>
> And within the workings of the world man can commit atrocities and murder or refrain from atrocities and murder. He is free to choose. But the universe goes on regardless. God is not a puppeteer pulling the strings and making man dance . . . God doesn't [necessarily] act to stop murder and He doesn't, on the other hand, encourage murder. The Holocaust . . . has nothing to do with God . . .

Some Christians say that the Holocaust was God's punishment for the Jews because many of them rejected Christ. However, the Bible states that we have all rejected Christ.[7]

If atrocity is necessarily a righteous punishment from God, why does 2 Timothy 3:12 state that "all that will live godly in Christ Jesus shall suffer persecution"?

When God tells us in the Bible that He punished someone with sickness or death, then we know that. But in the New Testament, Jesus Christ tells us that tragedy does not necessarily mean that God is punishing those involved. So, we are not free to conclude that tragedy is God's punishment.

In the next two chapters, we'll find some more Bible answers to the question of who causes atrocity.

Study Questions

1. Elie Wiesel wrote that the Holocaust "consumed his faith forever." On the other hand, many Christian martyrs testified before their deaths of the peace and power that God gave them. How can we be prepared to have our faith confirmed, not consumed, by atrocity?

2. One Holocaust survivor stated that we are on the earth to "be in God's service, to do God's bidding, to be God's people." How does that view sustain us in suffering?

3. List some Bible accounts or concepts that confirm that tragedy is not necessarily God's punishment on the sufferers.

---

7. See, for example, Isaiah 53 and Romans 3.

9

"The Faithful Were
In Anguish"

*Does God cause persecution, apostasy,
and abuse?*

From the 1530s to the 1620s, the Hutterian Brethren lived in large communities in Moravia, in what is now the Czech Republic. The Hutterian Brethren were Anabaptists who moved to Moravia from Switzerland, Austria, and other lands where they had been persecuted. In 1595, there were about one hundred Hutterian colonies, with an estimated total of 15,000 to 30,000 people.

Beginning in 1605, devastating wars plagued Moravia. Later, the opposing armies of the Thirty Years' War (1618-1648) crisscrossed the region, causing unspeakable suffering for these innocent Christians.

[1605] The faithful were in anguish about the atrocities committed by ungodly heathen against God-fearing, innocent people. It was appalling how they treated mothers with newborn babies, expectant mothers, and unmarried sisters. Most terrible of all was the way they ruthlessly carried off innocent little children, thrown on the horses' backs with feet bound together and head hanging down. Many mothers had to witness it. There was much weeping and heartache over all the brothers and sisters and boys and girls who were carried off. Husbands were separated from their wives, wives from their husbands, parents from children. . . . Now they were carried off to foreign lands and sold into slavery to cruel, sodomitic people. . . .

[1619] In these hard times, twelve of our communities were burned down and completely destroyed. . . . seventeen communities were plundered and desolated. But our greatest heartache was that forty men and women were cruelly murdered and that many God-fearing sisters, married and unmarried, were raped. . . .

[1620] At three o'clock that morning, when everyone was peacefully asleep in bed, a force . . . made a sudden and violent attack on Pribitz. They were so unrestrained, ungodly, and savage that within two or three hours they had murdered fifty-two brothers as well as a sister and her child. . . . To get money, the Poles tortured some brothers terribly. . . .

The attackers seriously injured about sixty more people, shooting, stabbing, beating, and slashing them so badly that many died afterward. . . .

In short, the way they treated the young and old, the crippled and sick, pregnant women, and mothers with newborn babies was so gruesome, devilish, and inhuman that such brutality had never happened in our land before. . . .

These and other unheard-of things that cannot be told for very shame were publicly committed by the imperial soldiers (who believed themselves to be the best of Christians). Anyone who has not himself known the anguish of hearing and seeing it all would not believe that a man who claims to be a Christian can commit acts so vile and devilish. It would have been no wonder if heaven itself had paled, if the earth had shaken, and if the elements had trembled. Even the devil might have shown greater fear of God's power and majesty than these devil-possessed men. . . .[1]

You can read the story in *The Chronicle of the Hutterian Brethren*. Page after page recounts the horrors of whole families and churches being extinguished in unimaginable brutality and lust. The *Martyr's Mirror*[2] contains many more accounts of innocent Christians being tortured and killed for their faith. Fathers and mothers were imprisoned, and the government sold their homes and properties and forced their children to live with other families or under the open sky. Many of these believers rotted in jails for months and years; many died in those conditions. Some lost their mental health. They were taunted, mocked, tricked, scorned.[3]

I wish no one would have to face such suffering or even hear that it exists. But I repeat this history here for one purpose: to show you that such deeds are precisely what the apostle Jude

---

1. Jacob Kleinsasser, editor-in-chief, *The Chronicle of the Hutterian Brethren, Volume 2* (Altona, Manitoba: Friesen Printers, 1998), pp. 161, 174, 177, 178, 186. Used by permission.
2. *Thieleman J. van Braght* (Scottdale, Pa.: Herald Press, 2001).
3. The Hutterites and Anabaptists, also known as defenseless Christians or rebaptizers, were persecuted because they did not follow the Catholic faith nor the Reformers of the 1500s such as Martin Luther. They believed that the Scriptures taught that only adults should be baptized upon confession of faith. They believed that the New Testament taught that Christians should not participate in war, and that Christians should live as Jesus taught in the Sermon on the Mount. For these reasons, they did not fit into the culture of the Middle Ages, and the mainline religions persecuted them. The Amish, Hutterites, and Mennonites are descendants of the Anabaptists.

is describing when he says that the Lord is coming "to execute judgment upon all, and to convince all that are ungodly among them of all their ungodly deeds which they have ungodly committed" (Jude 14, 15).

Why does Jude say that there are *ungodly* deeds if God ordains all deeds? Persecutors are not doing God's will in their atrocities against innocent Christians.

Why does the Bible say, "Behold, the devil shall cast some of you into prison" if God is causing persecution? God told the church at Pergamos that they live "where Satan's seat is," and commended them for being faithful when one of their brethren was martyred "where Satan dwelleth."[4]

God does not create people with the intention of exterminating them in unspeakable horror. Persecution is the devil's work. The persecutors are obeying Satan. They are living "contrary to sound doctrine; according to the glorious Gospel of the blessed God."[5] These people can do things to us that are not God's plan or will. Following Satan's will, they join him in killing Christians and making war with the remnant.[6]

Many happenings on earth are not good. God does not do them. "He that doeth good is of God; but he that doeth evil hath not seen God."[7]

Many happenings on earth are not just. God does not do them. "To crush under his feet all the prisoners of the earth, To turn aside the right of a man before the face of the most High, To subvert a man in his cause, the Lord approveth not."[8]

---

4. Revelation 2:10, 13
5. 1 Timothy 1:9-11
6. Revelation 12:11, 17
7. 3 John 11
8. Lamentations 3:34-36

Many happenings on earth are not righteous. God does not do them. "His work is honorable and glorious: and his righteousness endureth forever."[9]

Many happenings on earth are not merciful. God does not do them. The Bible says that God is "very pitiful, and of tender mercy."[10]

God "will not do iniquity."[11] "For thou art not a God that hath pleasure in wickedness: neither shall evil dwell with thee. . . . thou hatest all workers of iniquity."[12]

If God ordains everything that happens, He keeps people from His Word and causes apostasy.

In Cuba, a Christian lamenting the lack of Bibles in the country wrote this about their plight:

> . . . I also feel sad to see how in our country Christian bookstores, where churches can obtain the literature necessary as tools for our missionary labors and spiritual growth, do not exist. But God has determined it to be this way and His will is always good, pleasant, and perfect; and I accept it joyfully because he is God. . . .[13]

Was God keeping Bibles out of Cuba? Was this situation necessarily His will? Didn't Fidel Castro have a will? Doesn't Satan have a will?

The remainder of this letter describes plans to get more Bibles and Christian books into Cuba. But if God had "determined it to be this way", why should Christians work against His will?

---

9. Psalm 111:3
10. James 5:11
11. Zephaniah 3:5
12. Psalm 5:4, 5
13. *The Literature Lamplighter*, March-April 2015, p. 1.

On one hand, the writer is sad because of the lack of Bibles, but a few sentences later he accepts the situation joyfully as God's will. Do you see the tension—and the unbiblical view—that develops with this theology?

Suffering Christians sometimes face the same tension when well-meaning friends try to encourage them by saying that they should accept the circumstances God gave them. Often, this encouragement does not recognize that God does not give or plan all circumstances that we face. Responding to such encouragement, the parent of a wayward son replied,

> You say, "the portion that God, in His wisdom, gave us."
> Did God give this to us? Sometimes a minister will talk about God's will in relation to trials and I don't really feel the comfort they offer applies to me because it is not God's will for Kent to be like this. It's not His will that any should perish. If you can accept a trial as being God's will, that can bring a certain measure of comfort. But what if you know its not God's will?

It is never God's will that His children leave Him.[14] The greatest comfort we can give someone is not to assure them that their suffering or situation is necessarily from God, but that God is near to those who have broken hearts.[15]

If God ordains everything that happens, He plans and causes immoral abuse.

If your moral purity is violated, will you believe that God designed and planned that experience for you? After all God has said about immorality and how He hates it and will judge it, will you believe that God planned before your birth to cause you to be violated and defiled?

---

14. 2 Peter 3:9
15. Psalm 51:17

When a young girl worried about storms, danger, and death, her mother comforted her by telling her that love for God will cast out such fears.

> "If we love God, we love His will. If we love His will, we are not scared of His will. If we live for God, we may rest assured that nothing but His will shall happen in our lives, and if we have faith in His grace, there is nothing to fear."
>
> Lucy nodded thoughtfully. "I guess if we worry, we are either showing that we are scared of God's will or that we do not believe God's will is happening in our lives."
>
> "Exactly," agreed Mother. "And we cannot be scared of God's will if we realize that His will is always for the best of His children. God's ways are so much higher than our ways."[16]

Mother's reasoning is a classic example of how Christians leap from a Biblical truth to an unbiblical assumption. To love God and His will is certainly a mark of a true Christian. That far, Mother was correct. But when she stated, "If we live for God, nothing but His will shall happen in our lives," she overlooked that Satan makes war with Christians.[17] She overlooked that Satan has an ungodly will, and that God has given Satan a limited freedom to work iniquity.

Not recognizing Satan's work leads to two more common but unbiblical assumptions: Everything that happens to me is "for the best." If anything happens to me that does not seem "for the best," it is because I cannot understand God's ways.

So if Lucy is abducted by a kidnapper, is she to fearlessly ride away because she should not be "scared of God's will?" If Lucy is abused, is that God's will? If Lucy is killed for her faith, is that God's will? If it is God's will, why would He judge the perpetrators of such awful deeds forever in hell?

---

16. "Lucy's Worry Burrs," *The Christian Example*, May 9, 2010, p. 8.
17. Revelation 12:17

How much better the reply of another Christian mother when her daughter sought assurance that kidnapping would not happen to a Christian girl. "That can happen to anyone," her mother replied. "The devil does things in this world and God doesn't stop everything he does. But if you are a Christian, God will receive glory from your life even in that situation."

If we insist that God plans everything that happens and it is all "for good," we are simply living in a bubble. For example, take a young girl who has been abused as a child, and suffers physically, emotionally, and spiritually as a result. Where in the Scriptures does anyone get the authority to tell that girl, "What happened to you was all for the best. Now, to get to heaven, you must trust and obey the God who eternally planned to defile you and wreck your life."

How is anyone to trust a God who perpetrates such crimes? Do you see why people often go from believing that God plans and does everything to believing that there is no God at all?

Satan's will versus God's will

In picturesque language, Revelation describes the conflict that rages between God and Satan. Revelation 12 describes a woman (God's people) bringing to birth a man child (Jesus). Satan tries to devour Jesus as soon as He is born, but God marvelously protects the child.

A war broke out in heaven, as Michael and his angels fought the dragon and his angels. God won, and threw Satan and his angels out of heaven. God cast them to the earth, where for "a short time" Satan is raging at God's work and God's people. Satan kills some saints, but the "blood of the Lamb" gives them victory in spite of death. Satan persecutes the woman, but God gives her wings and nourishes her. Satan tries to drown her, but God makes the earth swallow up the flood.

In Revelation 13, Satan gives great power and authority to a beast who blasphemes God and deceives the world, while God gives greater power to those who are written in the book of life. Satan can kill them, but God gives them the "patience and faith of the saints." Their bodies suffer from Satan's will, but they are saved for a glorious eternity by God's will.

Over and over, Revelation describes things that Satan causes and things that God causes. If you take Revelation seriously, it is impossible to believe that everything that happens is God's will, God's plan, or the best thing that could happen.

In summary

To say that God causes all that happens means either that the devil is doing nothing or that he is doing God's will. Both are false. The story of Job does not say that God caused thieves to steal Job's animals and murder his herders. It does not say that God engineered a wind that blew down a house and killed all of Job's children. It says that *God permitted Satan* to exercise evil on Job's belongings and on his children.[18] What happened to Job was *Satan's will*, by God's permission.

The fact that God permits a thing does not mean:

- that it is His will.

- that it is the best thing that could happen.

- that He planned it or intended it.

- that He is pleased about it.

- that He chose it for us.

18. Job 1

God gave Satan and man wills and the power to exercise them. Their wills were given to them to make choices for God. But that means that they both had the possibility of choosing against God. Much of what we see in the world is the result of their opposition to God.

Depending on the situation you are facing, that may not seem like a satisfactory answer. But it is the answer the Bible gives us.

Real comfort

Perhaps you have taken comfort in the idea that no matter what has happened or will happen to you or anyone else, God planned it all. I want to lead you to a greater comfort.

The comfort of truth is far greater than the comfort of thinking that God plans and does everything. The truth is that though God allows Satan and ungodly people to cause much suffering for a limited time, yet He remains in final control of the world. He gives us strength to face anything that Satan brings to us, and He will someday deliver us from this fallen world to live with Him forever.

In Matthew 10, Jesus tells us that He was called Beelzebub, and we should expect the same label. We will be persecuted, but He will save us if we endure to the end. If we are faithful to Him, eternal joy and light will be ours. Is that small comfort?

There is more. Christ tells us not to fear those who kill us, because "the very hairs of your head are all numbered." Christ cares about each sparrow, but "ye are of more value than many sparrows." He is our companion in suffering. He will present us triumphantly to the Father. Is that small comfort?

Finally, Christ declares, "He that loseth his life for my sake shall find it." Is that small comfort?

No! This is the greatest comfort in the universe.

We are not alone in suffering. The Grieved One Himself suffered the fallenness of the world. He was murdered by His own creation. For what purpose? That He might give us a way out of the doom! That He might tell us with all His heart that He is with us in the gloom! That He might give us an eternity in the new heaven and new earth!

The cross of Jesus Christ is God's answer to the problem of evil and suffering. Christ died to guarantee that suffering and evil would someday end. He rose again and went to heaven to send the Comforter to us.[19]

> Lord should fear and anguish roll
> Darkly o'er my sinful soul,
> Thou who once was thus bereft
> That Thine own might ne'er be left,
> Teach me by that bitter cry
> In the gloom to know Thee nigh.[20]

Christ suffered so that we might never be alone when we suffer. Truly, as Frederick Faber wrote, "All this God is all for thee, a Father all thine own." Now *that* is real comfort.

In the 1980s, a church leader from United States visited fellow church members in a South American country suffering from guerrilla warfare. As the South Americans recounted the murders, mentioned the missing people, and told of looting and persecution, the American was horrified. Anguished, he finally cried, "Where was God when all this was happening?"

Astonished, the South Americans stared at him. "What do you mean?" they asked. "God was right here with us all the time!"

---

19. John 16:7
20. John Ellerton, 1871.

Study Questions

1. Recall Bible accounts and passages that teach us to expect persecution.

2. Why would God not be God if He caused apostasy?

3. What are ways to inspire trust and peace in our children as they become exposed to the world's violence?

4. Why is it an honor to be treated as Christ?

5. Explain how the cross of Jesus Christ answers the problem of evil and suffering.

10

"An Enemy Hath
Done This"

*Wheat and weeds do not come from
the same seed.*

An old German fable tells of an elderly man who lost confidence in God because of things he could not understand. He withdrew from society in despair and became a hermit, but God came to him in a dream. In the dream, a man offered to take him on a journey to restore his faith in the "ways of God."

The evening of their first day, the travelers stayed overnight with a man who was very thankful for what had happened that day. He had a neighbor who for years had held a grudge against

79

him. But that day the neighbor had come and made peace. As a token, he had given him a golden cup.

After a night's rest, the two men started out again. Imagine the hermit's consternation when his guide pulled out from under his garment the golden cup. After such a friendly welcome, and meal, and a bed, he had stolen the cup!

The hermit was filled with indignation at such treachery. But the guide, seeing his amazement, said, "Keep silence. These are the ways of God."

Again they traveled all day. By evening they were weary, dusty, and hungry. They arrived at the home of a family that was obviously very poor. But their host was nevertheless friendly and bade them come in and stay for the night.

The next morning as the two travelers started out, the guide tarried behind. The hermit turned to see where the guide was and saw to his horror that the house they had slept in was in flames! A deep suspicion and mistrust overcame him. He asked his mysterious guide if he had set fire to the house. The guide admitted that he had.

Again the hermit was filled with anger. He tried to withdraw from his guide, but again the guide told him, "Keep silence. These are the ways of God." Very reluctantly, he followed the guide.

"So these are the ways of God," thought the old man. "Impossible. God does not work in such a manner."

The next evening, they arrived at another dwelling. The owner allowed them inside, but he eyed them suspiciously. There was an air about him that made his guests ill at ease. They were almost afraid of him.

Playing on the floor at his feet was a young lad. As the host glanced at the boy, his face softened. It was plain to see that he thought highly of his little son, and it was also evident that he still had a soft spot in his heart.

The next morning the guide asked the host if the lad could accompany them to show them the way through the rough terrain ahead. At first the father refused, but then consented that the boy could go along as far as the river, and show them where to cross.

After a while they came to a waterfall. With a thundering roar, the water fell from a high cliff, spraying mist on the small footbridge that spanned the foaming water. The hermit crossed first. Looking back to see if the others were following, what should he see but the guide shoving the young lad into the torrent. The deafening roar of the falls drowned out the screams of the boy as he fell to his death in the rapids below.

Completely beside himself with indignation, the hermit shouted to the guide, "Not a step further will I go with you, for you are a devil."

The guide answered again, "Keep silence. These are the ways of God." Instantly, a heavenly light enveloped the guide and he was transformed into an angel. He began to speak, "I know you do not understand why I took the golden cup from our first host. I want you to know that the peace the neighbor pretended to make was false. The cup was poisoned. Had our host drunk from the cup, he would have died a miserable death. So I took the cup. Remember, God in His sovereignty sees the complete picture and He is always on time.

"As for our second host, under the ruins of his house lies buried a great treasure that he would never have found had not his house burnt. In clearing the ashes and preparing to rebuild, he will unearth the treasure."

"If the son of our last host had not drowned, he would have grown up to be a thief and a murderer like his father. Thus I have spared the young lad. The love that the thief had for his young son was the only soft spot in his heart. The pain of the tragedy will cause him to evaluate his life and seek God! So let it be known that God in all the things that you do not understand, has a good intention and motive."

The guide rose and disappeared into the heavens as an angel of God.[1]

---

1. Condensed from "Things Are Not Always As They Seem," *Family Life*, April 2013, pp. 7, 8.

What a fable! "Neither give heed to fables . . . which minister questions, rather than godly edifying which is in faith." To say that theft, arson, and murder are the ways of God contradicts the New Testament.[2]

A farmer knows wheat and weeds at sight. He knows that they did not come from the same seed.

When we assume that everything that happens is God's will, we are assuming that wheat and weeds come from the same seed. This destroys Christ's teaching that we can know good and evil at sight.

"Men don't believe in the devil now"

Why is it so popular to assume that God ordains all that is done? It is popular because the world does not want to believe that we are personally accountable for our actions. It is also popular because the world does not want to believe that Satan is real and powerful and can lead people to eternal damnation. But this is simply a rejection of reality, as Alfred J. Hough points out in the following poem.

> Men don't believe in the Devil now,
>   as their fathers used to do;
> They've forced the door of the broadest creed
>   to let his majesty through.
> There isn't a print of his cloven foot
>   or fiery dart from his brow
> To be found on earth or air today,
>   for the world has voted it so.
>
> Who dogs the steps of the toiling saint
>   and digs the pits for his feet?
> Who sows the tares in the fields of time
>   whenever God sows the wheat?

2.   1 Timothy 1:4

The Devil is voted not to be,
*   and of course, the thing is true;*
But who is doing the kind of work
*   that the Devil alone can do?*

We are told that he doesn't go about
*   as a roaring lion now.*
But whom shall we hold responsible
*   for the everlasting row*
To be heard in home, in church and state,
*   to the earth's remotest bound,*
If the Devil by unanimous vote
*   is nowhere to be found?*

Won't someone step to the front forthwith
*   and make their bow and show*
How the frauds and crimes of a single day
*   spring up? We want to know!*
The Devil was fairly voted out,
*   and of course, the Devil's gone;*
But simple people would like to know
*   who carries the business on?*

"An enemy hath done this"

Who carries the business on? Jesus tells us in the parable of the wheat and the tares that "an enemy hath done this."[3]

To believe that God ordains and causes everything that happens is not "strong faith." Instead, it is a result of Satan masquerading as God and deceiving people. The apostle Paul pleads with us, "Let no man deceive you by any means . . . the son of perdition; who opposeth and exalteth himself above all

---

3. Matthew 13:24-30

that is called God . . . he as God sitteth in the temple of God, shewing himself that he is God."[4]

The devil wants us to believe that *he* is God and that all he does is God's work. Don't fall for his lies! Wheat and weeds do not come from the same seeds. God allows Satan and his followers to work today, but someday God will destroy these evil ones "with the brightness of his coming."[5]

If we will bring the lost souls of this hurting, wicked world to Jesus Christ, we must recognize that God is the answer to, not the cause of, the wickedness of this world.

But doesn't Isaiah say that God causes evil?

"I form the light, and create darkness: I make peace, and create evil: I the Lord do all these things" (Isaiah 45:7). The New Testament states the same concept.

> For by him were all things created, that are in heaven, and that are in earth, visible and invisible, whether they be thrones, or dominions, or principalities, or powers: all things were created by him, and for him: And he is before all things, and by him all things consist (Colossians 1:16, 17).[6]

So if *all things* consist because of Christ, does evil exist because of Him? Yes! But how?

Because God is light, darkness can be identified. Because God is righteous, evil can be identified. Evil could not be known and could not exist if there was no God. Therefore, *God's holy existence defines and identifies evil.*

God created angels and people who could oppose Him. Therefore, *God created the possibility of evil.*

---

4. 2 Thessalonians 2:3,4
5. 2 Thessalonians 2:7-9
6. *Consist* here means *hold together* or *exist.*

That does not mean that evil is God's work or will. The New Testament says sin and perdition oppose all that is God.[7]

> In the face of evil, we ask the question, "How can God allow it?" The best answer to that is—God didn't make it!
>
> I have been an electrician for many years, and I have installed hundreds of lights. I put switches on all those lights. I do not remember anyone ever saying when I put in lights that I was creating darkness. Yet, when I put a switch on lights, I am producing darkness as well as light. But nobody says that I created darkness just because I gave them the ability to turn the lights off.
>
> But when God creates conditions by which the devil or mankind produces darkness, people say that the evil is God's fault. They aren't fair with God! God created everything good. Sin did everything else, and it still does. When people walk away from God they walk in darkness, but God did not create that darkness. God is where light is.
>
> Just because there is the ability to turn the lights off, just because there is the ability to not believe, we claim He created the darkness. Why? He is the Light! It is *we* who create the darkness; it is the *devil* who creates darkness. We do it when we walk away from the Light.[8]

> [God] set up the conditions that allowed evil to arise. This happened when God created Lucifer with the potential of serving Him or rebelling against Him. God did the same when He created Adam with the power to choose whether or not to eat the forbidden fruit. In both cases, evil was introduced when a creature acted in opposition to the Creator.
>
> Jesus said the the devil "is a liar, and the father of it" (John 8:44). The devil is also the ultimate father of all the evil in this world.[9]

---

7. 2 Thessalonians 2:3, 4

8. Edited excerpt from an unpublished sermon by Virgil Schrock, preached at Goodhue, Minnesota in October 2015.

9. Marvin Eicher, "I . . . Create Evil," *The Christian Contender*, December 2016, p. 187.

But doesn't Peter say that God wills persecution?

> For it is better, if the will of God be so, that ye suffer for well doing, than for evil doing (1 Peter 3:17).
>
> Wherefore let them that suffer according to the will of God commit the keeping of their souls to him in well doing, as unto a faithful Creator (1 Peter 4:19).

The Bible describes persecutors as against Christians and against God. For example, "men shall revile you, and persecute you, and shall say all manner of evil against you falsely, for my sake."[10] In other words, God says that because men are reviling Me, they are reviling you. If God caused persecution, He would be reviling Himself.

"Fear not them which kill the body, but are not able to kill the soul," Jesus said, "But rather fear him which is able to destroy both body and soul in hell."[11] Christ does not kill the body. He is, however, the final Judge.

In Christ's prayer for the church, He said that the world hates Christians because the world hates Him.[12] John stated, "The world knoweth us not, because it knew him not."

Paul says that persecutors "killed the Lord Jesus, and their own prophets, and have persecuted us; and they *please not* God, and are contrary to all men."[13]

Hebrews 12:3 describes the persecution of Christ as a "contradiction of sinners against himself." Christ did not contradict Himself, nor does He contradict His love and care for His people. God is not persecuting the church.

---

10. Matthew 5:10-11; see also Matthew 5:44.
11. Matthew 10:28
12. John 17:14
13. 1 Thessalonians 2:15, emphasis added.

In the verses at the beginning of this section, Peter is describing situations where people suffered because God allowed them to suffer, just as He allowed Job to suffer. Peter does not declare that God wills evil. In fact, he declares that "the face of the Lord is against them that do evil" (1 Peter 3:12).

God's will is that when we suffer, it should be for doing good, not for doing evil. God's will is that when we suffer, we should commit our souls to Him. That is what Peter means.

God commands us to pray for "a quiet and peaceable life in all godliness and honesty.[14] God does not command us to pray for peace while designing the opposite for us.

Real comfort

Perhaps you, like the hermit in the story, have taken comfort in the idea that everything that happens is God's will, yet you struggle to reconcile that with the Bible's teaching about God. The good news is that you don't need to reconcile those two ideas.

The title of this chapter is from Matthew 13, where Jesus clearly teaches that God does not do all that is done in the world. Right in God's own field, an enemy is sowing weeds. In the parable, God's servants assumed that God would want to immediately get rid of these weeds. They asked Him, "Wilt thou then that we go and gather them up?" But God told them that He would let good and evil grow together until the harvest, when He would punish the evil and gather the good.

Like the servants in the parable, we wish to rid the world of evil. For evil to grow in God's world seems contradictory. But since the evil is here, and since God does not root it out today,

---

14. 1 Timothy 2:2

many Christians assume that God planned the wickedness as well as the good. As the old fable teaches, many Christians even assume that God does bad things to accomplish good things.

Forget the fables! Evil exists because the devil is sowing wickedness and sinners are choosing wickedness. That God did not yet rid the world of evil means that He is waiting for the right time. This is not weakness; nor is it a hands-off Deity. This is omnipotent patience!

While we wait for the final harvest, we take great comfort in the fact that God is not causing "all things that offend, and them which do iniquity."[15] We can take great comfort that in spite of evil, Jesus Christ is redeeming repentant souls, cleansing them of wickedness, and turning them into beautiful wheat.

Someday, the angels will gather God's children away from the devil's wickedness and make them shine like the sun and the stars in a world that Satan can never touch.[16]

Study Questions

1. Why does the world resist believing in a literal Satan?

2. What are ways that the devil pretends to sit "in the temple of God shewing himself that he is God"?

3. Why is it inconsistent with the Bible to believe that God created evil in the same way that He created good?

4. It has been said, "We are living in the time of God's patience." What are some reasons the Bible gives for why God has not yet ended the world?

---

15. Matthew 13:41
16. Daniel 12:3; Matthew 13:43.

11

"I Won't Serve a God Who Sends Bears After Little Children"

Is God the author of bad harvests?

The cold Milwaukee wind fluttered the Gospel tract in my outstretched hand, and I smiled at the approaching pedestrian. "Sir, would you like to read a paper about God?" I asked. His eyes narrowed, and he turned to face me.

"No, I wouldn't." His voice was venomous. The words were icy pellets, spat with distaste. *"I won't serve a God who sends bears after little children."*

When we sin, God decrees that we suffer the consequences. Does that mean that He created death and other forms of suffering to punish us?

God made the law to protect us.

The fact that God is the Lawgiver does not make Him the author of the suffering that comes when we break those laws. For example, God's law of gravity helps to keep the universe and earth in order. Does that mean that if you fall from your house roof, God is responsible for the consequences? No . . . you are subject to law, and you are responsible. God did not make the law to hurt you; He made it to protect you. The fact that God created gravity does not make Him responsible for smashed heads.

A young man in a drunken stupor rolled off a yacht and drowned in a Los Angeles harbor. His lover, a Hollywood actress, was on television interview as the police investigators gave their findings. Grief-stricken, she turned to the camera and asked, "How could a loving God let this happen?"

She was asking the wrong question.

God created choice, but that does not make Him responsible for the evil that comes from bad choices.

God gave choice to the angels. Satan—fully rational, fully informed, and fully aware of God's beauty and holiness—chose to rebel. God isn't responsible for that.

God gave Adam and Eve choice, and they—rational, informed, and in full fellowship with God—chose to rebel. God isn't responsible for that.

God giving us choice is not like a parent putting a toddler out on a pier and walking off, saying, "I hope you make it!" The devil was not a toddler on a pier, and neither were Adam and Eve. Nor are you and I. We are rational, informed, and aware of God's standard of right and wrong. *We* are responsible for our choices.

Creating the law of sowing and reaping does not make God the author of bad harvests.

The Bible says that the harvest for good seed comes from God, and the harvest for bad seed comes from the devil.

"For he that soweth to his flesh shall *of the flesh* reap corruption; but he that soweth to the Spirit shall *of the Spirit* reap life everlasting."[1] If we sow to the flesh, we reap of the flesh. That reaping is bad because it is from the flesh. "For all that is in the world, the lust of the flesh, and the lust of the eyes, and the pride of life, is *not of the Father*, but is of the world."[2]

> For that they hated knowledge, and did not choose the fear of the Lord; they would none of my counsel: they despised all my reproof. Therefore shall they eat of the fruit of *their own way*, and be filled with *their own devices* (Proverbs 1:29-31, emphasis added).

The same principles are observed in Romans 1, where God describes people whom He gave up to evil because they chose to sin.

> Wherefore God also *gave them up* to uncleanness, through the lusts of their own hearts, to dishonour their own bodies between themselves. . . . For this cause God *gave them up* unto vile affections . . . men with men working that which is unseemly, and receiving in themselves that recompence of their error which was meet. And even as they did not like to retain God in their knowledge, God *gave them over* to a reprobate mind. (1:24-28; emphasis added).

God gave these people to vileness. Is He therefore the Creator of vileness? He gave them over to a reprobate mind. Is He

---

1. Galatians 6:8, emphasis added.
2. 1 John 2:16, emphasis added.

therefore the Creator of the reprobate mind? No, Peter says that the wicked "shall utterly perish in *their own* corruption."[3]

Paul tells us that when people do not love truth and take pleasure in unrighteousness, "God shall send them strong delusion, that they should believe a lie."[4] Does the fact that God sent these people delusions make Him the father of lies? No, John 8:44 says that the devil is the father of lying.

The same is true of dozens of other Bible stories. When God destroyed Sodom and Gomorrah, when He sent the plagues on Egypt, when He sent sickness, death, and famine to the erring Israelites, He was sending them to the fate that they willfully chose. God ordained the fate of the unbeliever, but He did not ordain anyone to be an unbeliever.

God created the law of sowing and reaping, but that does not make Him the Creator of the bad reaping. When a judge sentences a murderer to death, that judge is not a murderer. The judge is simply stating the law of sowing and reaping; the murderer is receiving his own harvest.

> The heathen are sunk down in the pit that they made: in the net which they hid is their own foot taken (Psalm 9:15).

Revelation 22:12 describes the final judgment in the same terms. When Jesus comes again, He will "give every man according as his work shall be."

God is the author of the law of sowing and reaping, but that does not make Him the Creator of the bad reaping.

"Your sins have withholden good things from you."

When Israel forgot God, He smote their children, withheld rain, and instigated war in their cities. When they followed

---

3.   2 Peter 2:12, emphasis added.
4.   2 Thessalonians 2:11

evil, they experienced evil. God told the Jews, "Thy way and thy doings have procured these things unto thee; this is thy wickedness, because it is bitter, because it reacheth unto thine heart" (Jeremiah 4:18).

At the end of the following passage, God stated exactly who was responsible for Israel's problems. They blamed God, but He replied:

> And it shall come to pass, when ye shall say, Wherefore doeth the LORD our God all these things unto us? then shalt thou answer them, Like as ye have forsaken me, and served strange gods in your land, so shall ye serve strangers in a land that is not yours. . . .
>
> Fear ye not me? saith the LORD: will ye not tremble at my presence . . .
>
> *Your iniquities have turned away these things, and your sins have withholden good things from you.* . . . Shall I not visit for these things? saith the LORD: shall not my soul be avenged on such a nation as this? (Jeremiah 5:19, 22, 25, 29, emphasis added).

If a sinner refuses pardon, all that is left for him is the fruit of his own choice: suffering, destruction, death, and God's wrath.

God uses evil to avenge evil.

God is intimately involved in making justice happen. He "spared not the old world, but saved Noah the eighth person, bringing in the flood upon the world of the ungodly; And turning the cities of Sodom and Gomorrha into ashes condemned them with an overthrow, making them an ensample unto those that after should live ungodly."[5] "Vengeance is mine, I will repay, saith the LORD."[6]

---

5. 2 Peter 2:5, 6
6. Romans 12:19

In many ways, God's vengeance uses the evil Satan and man brought into the world to judge sinful man. For example, Genesis 6:11 and 13 say that the earth was "filled with violence"—a fact which displeased God exceedingly. Yet God often uses humanity's violence to judge nations and restrain sinners.

> "Thy right hand, O LORD, hath dashed in pieces the enemy" (Exodus 15:6).

> "O Assyrian, the rod of mine anger, and the staff in their hand is mine indignation" (Isaiah 10:5).

> "I have created the waster to destroy" (Isaiah 54:16).

> "Thus saith the LORD of hosts, . . . Behold, I will send and take Nebuchadrezzar the king of Babylon, my servant, . . . And when he cometh he shall smite the land of Egypt, and deliver such as are for death to death; and such as are for captivity to captivity, and such as are for the sword to the sword" (Jeremiah 43:10-11).

> "I will punish you for all your iniquities . . . shall there be evil in a city, and the LORD hath not done it?" (Amos 3:6).

The Bible clearly teaches that God executes judgment *and* that sinners bring evil on themselves. These facts are compatible; they happen at the same time. Psalm 9:16 states, "The LORD is known by the judgment which he executeth: the wicked is snared in the work of his own hands." Daniel makes the same point: "Neither have we obeyed the voice of the LORD our God . . . Therefore hath the LORD watched upon the evil, and brought it upon us."[7] The fact that God uses evil to judge evil exalts Him. It does not diminish His role.

When God uses evil to judge evil, does that make the evil good? For example, was the catastrophe at Sodom and

---

7. Daniel 9:10, 14

Gomorrah good? Certainly, justice is good. But God does not confuse the issues by calling bad things *good*, even when He does them. Almost invariably, God uses words such as *holy*, *righteous*, *just*, and *true* to describe His acts of justice. We should follow the same pattern.

The fact that God uses evil to judge evil exalts Himself. It does not mean that evil is good or that God brought it into the world originally.

But what about children that suffer when their parents are judged? It is not *their* sin that withholds good from them.

In Hosea 13:16, God told the Israelites, "Samaria shall become desolate; for she hath rebelled against her God: they shall fall by the sword: *their infants shall be dashed in pieces*, and their women with child shall be ripped up" (emphasis added).

What kind of God would allow that to happen to innocent infants?

The God who made parents responsible for children. If godly parents can bless their children, then sinful parents can bring evil on their children. The fate of children is usually closely tied to the character of their parents. When evil comes to children because of their sinful parents, God will judge those parents for what they brought to their children. He will also give those children an opportunity to inherit eternal life.

The God who is so merciful that he gave the corrupt Old Testament societies (including the Jews) hundreds of years to repent. God did not judge those cultures until He had exhausted every opportunity to save them.

In Hosea 13 and 14, God pleads with Israel to turn from their wicked ways and be saved. All of God's warnings are interspersed with offers of forgiveness—if only the Israelites would love Him and obey Him. God did not want them to fall by the sword. God did not want their infants to be dashed in pieces. But if they persisted in evil, God Himself could not save them from the law of sowing and reaping.

But when God sent bears after little children . . . is this really a case of fair judgment on sin?

> And [Elisha] went up from thence unto Bethel: and as he was going up by the way, there came forth little children out of the city, and mocked him, and said unto him, Go up, thou bald head; go up, thou bald head.
>
> And he turned back, and looked on them, and cursed them in the name of the Lord. And there came forth two she bears out of the wood, and tare forty and two children of them (2 Kings 2:23, 24).

The late Christian apologist Norman L. Geisler often came up against this issue in debates with atheists and skeptics. He pointed out that Hebrew scholars believe that "little children" in the original language can be translated "young people." They likely compare to a modern street gang of dangerous teenagers.

These young people were not just making fun of a bald man; they were challenging whether Elisha was God's prophet. They held him in contempt, and they reaped what they sowed. Whatever their age, these "little children" were old enough to be personally responsible for what they did. They were old enough to understand God's judgment on their mocking.

"Is the law sin? God forbid."

Throughout this chapter I have stated repeatedly that being the author of the law of sowing and reaping does not make God the author of evil and death. I want to clinch that point with Paul's powerful statements in Romans 7.

There Paul states that he became aware of sin because of the law. But instead of concluding that for sin to exist, God must have created it, he states the opposite. God's law is holy, and sin is "another law" that wants to steal me away from God.

> Is the law sin? God forbid. . . . when the commandment came, sin revived, and I died. And the commandment, which was ordained to be unto life, I found to be unto death.
>
> For sin, taking occasion by the commandment, deceived me, and by it slew me.
>
> Wherefore the law is holy, and the commandment holy, and just, and good.
>
> Was then that which is good made death unto me? God forbid. But sin, that it might appear sin, working death in me by that which is good; that sin by the commandment might become exceeding sinful. . . . If then I do that which I would not, I consent unto the law that it is good. . . .
>
> I find then a law, that, when I would do good, evil is present with me. For I delight in the law of God after the inward man: But I see another law in my members, warring against the law of my mind, and bringing me into captivity to the law of sin which is in my members.
>
> O wretched man that I am! who shall deliver me from the body of this death? I thank God through Jesus Christ our Lord (Romans 7:7, 9-13, 16, 21-25).

There is the truth. Sin and evil are another law—not God's law. The law of sin and evil opposes God. It fights His goodness and holiness. It holds man captive to a body of death.

"I thank God through Jesus Christ our Lord"

The real problem in all this is not theological. It is intensely practical. The law of sowing and reaping would carry us helplessly to judgment were it not for the love of Jesus Christ. Every one of us faces the possibility that our own choices to sin could hand us over to our implacable enemy.

What is the solution? What is our comfort? It is deliverance through Jesus Christ. The overwhelming condemnation that we all face as violators of God's law is removed when we come to Christ and "walk not after the flesh, but after the Spirit."

We still suffer from choices we made when we were sinners. God does not miraculously lift imprisoned criminals from their cells when they repent. Our old life in sin forms habits that cause us much grief as Christians. But we are totally saved from eternal death. That is not because the law of sowing and reaping has been ignored, bypassed, or invalidated, but because it has been justly satisfied for us by the lifeblood of the perfect Lamb of God.

Study Questions

1. What are some similarities between the law of gravity and the law of sowing and reaping?

2. God created the law of sowing and reaping, but did not create bad harvests. Explain.

3. Why do many innocent children suffer?

4. List some Scripture passages that give you joy in spite of the fact that you suffer from past sinful choices.

12

"I Don't Want the Devil to Put Me in My Grave"

Does God cause people to die?

I don't want the devil to put me in my grave!" Ruby cowered in the corner of her sofa, waving her arms toward a shadowy corner near the ceiling. "When I am in bed, the devil comes after me, trying to get me!"

Ruby was elderly, frail, and alone. She was facing the end of her life, and she was desperately afraid. It took her a long time to calm down that night, but she listened to the message of hope in Jesus Christ, and eventually prayed with us, asking God to forgive her sins and take care of her.

When Ruby went to the grave, God was with her. She went through the valley of the shadow of death, but even as she did,

God prepared a table for her in the presence of her enemies. They were vanquished. She was His!

But who did put Ruby in her grave? Does God cause us to die? Does He decide when we die? When we die, does that mean that God had nothing more for us to do on earth?

God gives human life, and He can take human life.

Hannah rejoiced in the birth of her son, proclaiming, "The LORD killeth, and maketh alive."[1] But this verse does not mean that God kills and makes alive without regard to human choice.

> Supposedly everyone's death is scheduled and executed by God. How then are we to think when a drunkard dies young as a consequence of his drinking? Is that not a premature death? Did not his choices hasten the day of his death? Did God will that he should die as quickly as he did? By the same token we could ask—is every suicide a divinely-scheduled death?
>
> And yes, "He maketh alive." But He does not do so without human instruments. Suppose, for example, a couple deliberately remains childless. Does God in that instance still "make alive?" It is obvious that outcomes are determined somewhat by the choices of free moral agents.[2]

In the Great Flood, God took life because man was wicked continually. The Lord "smote all the firstborn in the land of Egypt.[3] In Deuteronomy 32, Moses told the Jews of God's vengeance on sin, including this declaration: "I kill, and I make alive; I wound, and I heal: neither is there any that can deliver out of my hand."

God is sovereign over human life, but He is not the cause of all death. In the Bible accounts where God takes human life, it was almost always because people resisted God long and arrogantly, or because they disobeyed God's commands.[4]

---

1. 1 Samuel 2:6
2. Personal letter from Merle Ruth, October 23, 2008. Used by permission.
3. Exodus 12:29
4. See Ezekiel 24:16-18 for an instance when God took the life of an apparently righteous person for a specific prophetic sign.

God does not take the life of all the people who die.

God did not kill Abel. Cain did. God did not kill Uriah. King David did by sending him to a position where he was certain to die. God did not kill Naboth. Ahab did. God did not kill Zechariah the son of Jehoiada the priest. King Joash did.

It was not God's will for Abel, Uriah, Naboth, and Zechariah to die when they died. God took vengeance on those who caused their deaths. Just because God lets someone die when he is killed does not mean that God willed the death. If all death is God's will, murder would not exist.

That is Biblical reality, yet Christians routinely slip into fatalism, as the following accounts illustrate.

As a Pakistani Christian was fleeing his persecutors, he was not worried about the bullets blazing after him. "The bullet meant for you cannot miss you," he said, "And the bullet not meant for you cannot hit you." If that was true, why did he flee?

Maybe you have heard this line, "What if a bad man shoots a Christian in the prime of life, a young father, or a minister in the church? Was God finished with that man on earth?"

"Yes," the reasoning goes, "God wanted him in heaven, or he wouldn't have been killed." But this reasoning does not reckon with the fact that God allows some things that are not His will, even in the lives of His children.[5]

God does not take the life of all the people who die. The fact that God allows someone to die does not mean that He chose to take their life at that time, or that He had nothing more for them to do on earth.

---

5. Notice Jesus' descriptions of persecutions and murders of saints in Matthew 23:29-37.

Is death a divine appointment?

When someone dies, it is often said that they reached the day appointed for their death.

But the Bible says that "bloody and deceitful men shall not live out half their days."[6] It is obvious, then, that these people do not live as long as they could have. People who commit suicide also do not live as long as they otherwise would have. People can thwart God's will for their lives.

What about the innocent victims of wanton carelessness, violence, and warfare? Because they did not take their lives into their own hands, do they always die in God's "appointed time?" Does God allow people to thwart His will for other people's lives?

Yes, He does. God did not want sixty-eight of Gideon's sons to die by their brother's hand. God did not want eighty-five priests and their wives and children to fall in one day by Doeg's sword. Today, God does not want precious lives lost in the terrible shootings and bombings occuring in schools, churches, and grocery stores.

These victims did not die in their supposed "appointed time." They died when their murderers disobeyed God's will.

But doesn't the Bible say that God appoints the day of death?

Hebrews 9:27 states that "it is appointed unto men once to die." Fallen man is appointed to die once. Ecclesiastes 8:8 states the same truth: "There is no man that hath power over the spirit to retain the spirit; neither hath he power in the day of death: and there is no discharge in that war." These passages do not necessarily imply that God decrees the time and manner of a person's death.

---

6. Psalm 55:23

Job 14:5 states that man's "days are determined, the number of his months are with thee, thou hast appointed his bounds that he cannot pass." Since God has told us that choices and circumstances can change how long people live, this verse seems to explain the same truth as Psalm 90:10 and Job 7:1.

> The days of our years are threescore years and ten; and if by reason of strength they be fourscore years . . . it is soon cut off, and we fly away.
> Is there not an appointed time to man upon earth? are not his days also like the days of an hireling?

These verses appear to describe average lifetimes, not a specific number of days for each individual.

God has set the average bounds of the human lifespan, but this does not mean that God has appointed each person's day or manner of death.

Our experiences and actions can directly influence life and death.

War, climate, hygiene, genetics, exercise, and diet affects life spans. When a heart attack patient receives rapid medical care, it often saves his life; without it, he usually dies. Good medical care and vaccines greatly reduce child deaths. Caution reduces workplace injuries and deaths.

None of this means that man is sovereign over life. But it does mean that God has established many ways by which we can influence our lifespan. He expects us to choose, within our ability, to lengthen our lives and the lives of those in our care.

If I could save a drowning man but do not, I am responsible for his death. Proverbs says, "If thou forbear to deliver them that are drawn unto death, and those that are ready to be slain; If thou sayest, Behold, we knew it not; doth not he that pondereth the heart consider it? . . . and shall not he render to every man according to his works?" (24:11-12).

If I know my bull is dangerous and I do not keep him away from people, I am responsible if the bull kills someone.[7] My actions can directly influence life and death.

· *God is sovereign over life and death. In His sovereignty, He allows our choices, as well as circumstances beyond our control, to influence the time and manner of our death.*

"Now let me die"

After Jacob met his long-lost son Joseph, he said, "Now let me die."[8] Seventeen years later, "the time drew near that [Jacob] must die." Within a few weeks, perhaps, Joseph heard that his father was sick, and went to see him. Later yet, "when Jacob had made an end of commanding his sons, he gathered up his feet into the bed, and yielded up the ghost, and was gathered unto his people."

To me, this describes an experience in which God is deeply involved, though He allows the processes of the Fall to take their toll on our bodies. Jacob said, "Now let me die," not "now take my life." His old age, weariness, and sickness made it obvious that it was time to go. When life in a fallen body on a fallen earth had carried Jacob to the point of death, he asked God to let him go and he yielded his body to death.

Though God lets us die through a variety of circumstances He did not cause, He is still in control. He is a very present help in the time of trouble, and especially at the time of death. "The eternal God is thy refuge, and underneath are the everlasting arms."[9]

---

7. Exodus 21:28-30
8. Genesis 46:30
9. Dueteronomy 33:27

"God sees the little sparrow fall."

Whenever and however we die, God is with us. Even a sparrow does not fall without His notice![10] God does not promise to save our bodies from harm, but He promises to redeem our souls from violence.[11] No matter how we die, our deaths are "precious in the sight of the LORD."[12] What comfort!

On the other hand, the idea that God has selected the way I will die is not all that comforting. How comforting would it be to think that God selects abortion for millions of babies each year? How comforting would it be to think that God selects cancer, starvation, abuse, gunshots, burning, crushing, dismemberment, and drowning for millions of people each year? There is no comfort in those thoughts because God is not the source of those things. Satan is the source of those things, and there is no comfort in Satan.[13]

Real comfort is that God has "not appointed us to wrath, but to obtain salvation by our Lord Jesus Christ."[14] Real comfort is that if I walk with Him, He will walk with me through the valley of death. I need not fear evil because He is stronger than evil and will carry me beyond its reach forever.

That Christ will carry me through the valley of death is far more important than the circumstances that cause my death. The idea that God plans the time and circumstances of all deaths is a misguided obsession with death. How and when we die is of little significance. However, whether we are walking with Christ when we die is of great significance.

---

10. Matthew 10:29-31
11. Psalm 72:14, see also Matthew 10:28 and Luke 12:4.
12. Psalm 116:15
13. Ephesians 2:2
14. 1 Thessalonians 5:9-11

So what put Ruby in her grave? Sin! "By one man sin entered into the world, and death by sin; and so death passed upon all men."[15]

And who will lift Ruby from her grave? The Lord Jesus Christ! "That as sin hath reigned unto death, even so might grace reign through righteousness unto eternal life by Jesus Christ our Lord."[16]

Study Questions

1. Why would the concept of murder not exist if all deaths were God's will?

2. Does God ever allow sinners to thwart His will for the physical lives of Christians?

3. List some ways by which God allows people to influence their own life spans.

4. Why should we be concerned about safety and responsive to emergencies?

5. What is our real comfort in the time of death?

---

15. Romans 5:12
16. Romans 5:21

13

Why Death Makes
the Earth Flat

What God says about death

A young boy was killed in a tragic accident. Reflecting on his death, his father remarked, "I can see why God did it. I was not a strong Christian at the time, and I believe God took my son's life so that I would grow closer to Him. Life is so much better now than it was before his death. I am grateful to God for bringing that experience into my life, and I would not have it any other way."

Praise God for the spiritual strength that comes from walking with Him through tragedies. However, there are thousands of Christians who are never able to say of a death or other tragedy in their lives, "I am grateful that God brought that experience into my life, and I would not have it any other way." I am one of them. We still long to have our loved ones with us. If we could, we would have it another way.

Is that weak faith? To be a strong Christian, do you have to believe that everything in the world is exactly the way God wants it, and you must accept it as His good plan?

Do you know that God Himself would rather have the world without tragedies? God Himself would rather have the world another way.

I want to show you in this chapter how God describes death. But before that, read this story.

Why death makes the earth flat.

Father is dead. It was Cornelia's first thought every morning. Each time it was like a new shock, completely unreal and horrible.

She seemed to have broken into several pieces. One part of her was numb, frozen. Part of her moved, and answered questions, and worked, and—sometimes—swallowed food. But her other self, her real self, was like a lost child groping its way through a dark tunnel where no light ever shines. Nothing but bewilderment and pain were there.

Mother and the boys all cried a lot. Johann in the barn, with his face against the harness where Father hung it last. Anton when he started out to school again where a new teacher waited for him. Mother at any time of day, but most of all at night. . . .

"Won't you write a letter to Agatha?" she coaxed one day. . . . "Agatha will want to hear everything. . . . All the details. Especially from her very own sister. Think. If *you* were so far away now!"

So Cornelia got out the writing materials, and sat down at the kitchen table.

"Manitoba, Canada. Dec. 2, 1877.

Dear Agatha! By now you will have heard that Father died. . . .

She stared at the words. Dead. Dead. Father's dead. It was like a wave of seasickness washing over her.

"I can't write," she announced, her voice cracking.

"Try, Cornelia."

She took a fresh grip on her pen. . . . "Do you remember, Agatha, how I used to make fun of Martha because she thought the earth was flat? Well, it is. It's flat, I tell you. *Flat*. There is no shape. There is nothing beautiful. There is no meaning to anything. Father is dead—and it's not *right* that he should be dead. He was good and gentle and wise. He taught people to love God. But why should I love God if He does horrible things like this? Why? Tell me, why? The very worst thing that can happen has happened . . . ."

The words were coming fast now. Cornelia's pen stabbed the paper. Her breath came in shivering gusts.

Mother, sitting opposite, said, "May I read?"

"There." Cornelia shoved the sheet across the table.

"Ach, my child! My poor child!" whispered Mother. Her face dropped to her folded hands. In the long silence Cornelia could hear heavy drops dripping onto the oilcloth table cover.[1]

Do you know what it is for the earth to be flat? To have no shape? To wonder why you should love God, or even to wonder if God exists? Death can do that to stalwart Christians.

Death makes the earth flat because God did not make us to die. He made us to live and walk with Him forever. We die, not because of God's will, but because of *man's* will. "By one man sin entered into the world, and death by sin; and so death passed upon all men" (Romans 5:12).

Death is not good. Death is not glorious. God did not create death. Death is not God's perfect will. In fact, death is the opposite of God. God is impatient to destroy death!

---

1. Margaret Epp, *The Earth Is Round* (Winnipeg, Manitoba: Kindred Press, 1974), pp. 216-218. Used by permission.

Death is Satan's most supreme blow against the image of God in us. Death contradicts our God-given spirit of life. That is why the earth is flat when our loved ones die. When Cornelia wrote, "Father is dead—and it is not *right* that he should be dead," she was face to face with this contradiction.

In picturesque language, the Bible further explains why death is such a blow, such a contradiction to the nature of our Creator, and such a difficult thing for us to face.

"The power of the dog"

King David called death "the power of the dog" and "the lion's mouth." In the Bible, *dog* describes enemies of God's people—think Goliath and Jezebel. Jesus told us to not to give holy things "unto the dogs." Paul said, "Beware of dogs." Revelation 22 assures us that the dog's power cannot enter heaven.[2]

The dog is the devil and his servants, and death is their power. That is why Jesus told the mob who came to capture and crucify Him, "This is your hour, and the power of darkness."[3] But the dog of death has only one hour. He will soon lie eternally coiled in his own snare.[4]

The tension that you and I feel about death is because death is the dog's device, and we are children of the Lamb.

"The land of the enemy"

Herod the Great senselessly murdered Bethlehem's baby boys, just to remove one child who was supposedly a threat to his throne.[5] Rachel wept for her children, Matthew 2:18 says, "and would not be comforted, because they are not."

2. Matthew 7:6; Psalm 22:20, 21; Philippians 3:2
3. Luke 22:53
4. Revelation 18:10, 17-20.
5. Matthew 2:16

Jeremiah 31 has a beautiful prophecy for those bereaved families. Did God tell them that this tragedy was all for the best? Did He tell them that they would understand it all by and by? Did He tell them it was a divine appointment? No!

He told them the truth about death. He told them that their children were in the land of the enemy, but He promised that He would bring them back.

> Thus saith the LORD; Refrain thy voice from weeping, and thine eyes from tears: for thy work shall be rewarded, saith the LORD; and they shall come again from the land of the enemy. And there is hope in thine end, saith the LORD, that thy children shall come again to their own border.

Were these little children safe in God's care? Absolutely. But were they where they would have been if God's will had been followed? No! Had God's will been done, they would have been snuggled in their mothers' arms. Had God's will been done, they would have been riding on their daddys' shoulders.

God allowed these children to die, but the deaths were not His will. He is eternally angry with those child murderers if they have not repented, because they defied His will.

The little children of Bethlehem are gone because of the will of the enemy. They are gone because of "him that had the power of death, that is, the devil."[6] To their parents *and* to God, it was not their "time to go." But it was the time they went, because of the enemy.

"Death is a thief," said a friend of mine who lost his father at age fifteen. "Death stole from me what every boy needs, and I am not reconciled to the robber."

The tension that you and I feel about death is because death is the enemy of God and mankind.

---

6. Hebrews 2:14

Darkness and the shadow of death

Darkness, sin, and death go together throughout the Bible. In his misery, Job spoke of "darkness and the shadow of death." He called going to the grave "making my bed in the darkness." King David was comforted that God was with him in the "shadow of death, and rejoiced that God could fill hungry souls that lived "in darkness and in the shadow of death." Jesus Christ came to rescue people sitting in "darkness . . . in the region and shadow of death." God describes hell as the chains of darkness and an eternal mist of darkness.[7]

The tension we feel about death is because death is the power of darkness, and we are "not of the night, nor of darkness."[8]

Death is corruption.

"All flesh shall perish together," Job mourned, "and man shall turn again unto dust." Jonah rejoiced that God had brought his life back from corruption, and one of the proofs of Christ's divinity was that "his soul was not left in hell [the grave], neither did his flesh see corruption."[9]

"So when this corruptible shall have put on incorruption, and this mortal shall have put on immortality," Paul exulted, "then shall be brought to pass the saying that is written, Death is swallowed up in victory."[10]

Corruption is not the will of our incorruptible God. He did not make our flesh to perish; He made us to live forever. "Him that had the power of death, that is, the devil"[11] brought corruption, dishonor, and weakness into the world.

7. Job 3:5; Job 17:13; Psalm 23:4; Psalm 107:10; Matthew 4:16
8. 1 Thessalonians 5:5
9. Job 34:15; Jonah 2:6; Acts 2:31
10. 1 Corinthians 15:54
11. Hebrews 2:14

God will swallow up this corruption in victory! He did not make it, and He will not allow it to plague us forever.

The tension that we feel about death is because death means corruption and dishonor for our earthly bodies.

"O death, I will be thy plagues"

Here is the most powerful evidence that death was not God's design for us. The Bible calls death God's enemy, and God states, "The last enemy that shall be destroyed is death."[12]

When God states that death is an enemy that must be destroyed, it is obvious that He did not create death. God's enemies are a result of angels and men leaving the very good state in which God created them. Death was not part of God's plan—it was the result of violating God's plan.

For thousands of years, God has warned death that He will destroy it.

> And he will destroy in this mountain the face of the covering cast over all people, and the vail that is spread over all nations. He will swallow up death in victory; and the Lord God will wipe away tears from off all faces; and the rebuke of his people shall he take away from off all the earth: for the Lord hath spoken it (Isaiah 25:7-8).

> I will ransom them from the power of the grave; I will redeem them from death: O death, I will be thy plagues; O grave, I will be thy destruction: repentance shall be hid from mine eyes (Hosea 13:14).

> Forasmuch then as the children are partakers of flesh and blood, he also himself likewise took part of the same; that through death he might destroy him that had the power of death, that is, the devil.

> And deliver them who through fear of death were all their lifetime subject to bondage (Hebrews 2:14, 15).

12. 1 Corinthians 15:26

> But now is made manifest by the appearing of our Saviour Jesus Christ, who hath abolished death, and hath brought life and immortality to light through the gospel (2 Timothy 1:10).

John 11:33 says Jesus "groaned in the spirit" over Lazarus' death. In the Greek, that wording means that Jesus was deeply angry about the death, not merely responding with mild emotion. James Strong's first definition for that Greek word is to snort with anger. Jesus Christ is angry with the devil, who holds the power of death.

One day soon God will force death to deliver up its victims—and then God will throw it into the lake of fire. For the innocent and for God's people, there will be no more death.[13]

God's impatience to destroy death is mirrored in our own reluctance to accept death.

So how should we relate to death?

Because God is angry at death and determined to destroy it, should we rage and scream at death? Should we grow bitter and morose and lose hope because this enemy of God causes so much pain?

On the other hand, because God allowed death, should we honor death as the way of God? Should we portray God as the One who takes all human life? Should we believe that death is God's very good plan?

The Scriptures answer these questions.

God's image within us calls us to resist death within our ability to do so. God wants us to practice safety, use medical knowledge, and solve dangerous situations as far as we can. He gave us the will to live and to save life.

---

13. Revelation 20:13, 14; 21:4

God's Word tells us that ultimately, we do not have the power to avoid death. When we have done His will in an effort to preserve our lives and the lives of others, we will still face death until God finally abolishes death. We accept that as the result of the Fall of man, not as God's very good plan for us. We accept death as an inevitable result of Satan's will and man's will, not as God's original design for us. Yet we stand with our God in identifying death as an enemy, a rebuke, a bondage, and the ultimate evidence of Satan's destructive hatred for us.

What does God do with His burning desire to destroy death and ransom us from the grave? All through history, He made a way for people to be saved from eternal death. He "laid down His life for us."[14] He delivered us from the fear of death. He pities; He loves; He calls; He pleads; He redeems; He saves!

What will you do with your God-given tension about death? Follow God's example! Lay down your life for others. Open your arms with compassion. Pity, love, call, plead, sacrifice! Build up yourself, Jude says,

> "on your most holy faith, praying in the Holy Ghost, keep yourselves in the love of God, looking for the mercy of our Lord Jesus Christ unto eternal life. And of some have compassion, making a difference: And others save with fear, pulling them out of the fire; hating even the garment spotted by the flesh."[15]

That is what God wants us to do with our tension about death. Not to lose it, but to use it. Not to abandon Him, but to stand with Him. Not to honor death, but to honor Him. God wants us to channel our tension about death . . . into Life!

---

14. 1 John 3:16
15. Jude 20-23

The death of death

Dear friends, there is little comfort in the idea that death is God's will, design, and plan. There is little comfort in that because God Himself has told us that death is His avowed enemy. Do not blame Him for what He did not do. Instead, praise Him for saving us from what He did not do!

The real comfort in death is this: Christ's terrible moment on the cross abolished death. The icy grip of death is breaking. The eternal spring of immortality is budding.[16]

The One who is "the resurrection and the life" will hold death's funeral, and the service has already begun.

The death of death! The prison doors flung open! Our children racing for our arms! Our mothers and fathers, wives and husbands, whole and happy! Come, Lord Jesus!

Study Questions

1. Why does death make the earth seem flat?

2. Explain how our difficulty in facing death is a reflection of God's nature.

3. Contrast the God-given fear of death with the unbeliever's terror of death.

4. What does God want us to do with our tension about death?

5. Why is the icy grip of death already breaking?

---

16. Colossians 2:14, 15

14

Did God Plan the Death of My Dad?

And other questions about death

On January 7, 1956, Nate Saint, Roger Youderian, Pete Fleming, Ed McCully, and Jim Elliot were speared to death as they tried to evangelize the Waodani tribe of the Aucas in Ecuador. Elizabeth Elliot, Jim's widow, told the story in *Through Gates of Splendor*.[1] For Steve Saint, Nate's son, it is not just a story. It is real life.

Steve was only five years old when his mother called him into her bedroom and told him that his dad had died. It broke his heart that his dad was never coming home, and that he had not taken them all along to be with Jesus.

---

1. Elisabeth Elliot, (Carol Stream, Il.: Tyndale House Publishers, 1956).

As Steve grew up, however, the Waodani people opened their hearts to the Gospel, and amazing changes took place in their tribe. Beyond that, the sacrifice of those five men challenged countless people to follow Christ more fully, and thousands of missionaries name those deaths as the event that moved their hearts to respond to God's call.

Over the years, Steve came to believe that the Lord planned his dad's death. When others objected to that conclusion, he pointed to the fact that God, in His "determinate counsel and foreknowledge," delivered Christ to his murderers. He concluded, "Don't anybody tell me this can't be. If God could plan the death of His own righteous Son, why couldn't He plan the death of my dad?"[2]

We will come back to Steve's question at the end of this chapter. Let's consider a few other questions first.

Job said, "the LORD gave, and the LORD hath taken away." Doesn't that mean that God created Job's calamities?

Job did not know what was going on behind the scenes. One reason that God gave us the book of Job was to tell us what is going on behind the scenes when we face calamity.

When God told Satan, "Behold, all that he hath is in thy power," Satan went out from the presence of the Lord and began to trouble Job.

Theft, murder, fire, and the deaths of Job's children all came from Satan.

Satan wanted to trouble Job further, and God said, "Behold, he is in thine hand; but save his life." Job's boils came from Satan.

---

2. *Suffering and the Sovereignty of God*, ibid., p. 117. Used by permission.

Now, God told Satan in Job 2:3, "Thou movedst me against him, to destroy him without cause." Does that mean that God was causing this destruction?

No, it simply means that without God's permission, Satan could not trouble Job. Several times, Satan taunted God, "Put forth your hand and touch Job, and he will curse you." God always replied, "Behold, he is in *your* hand and *your* power." Why did God emphasize that? He emphasized it so that we would understand that while He allowed Job to be tested, all the evil Job faced was from Satan. Allowing the evil to come to Job did not make God the author or planner of the evil.

Job was the focus of the great battle between God and Satan. You and I are too. God wants to prove our faith and show Satan that His followers are genuine. Satan wants to prove to God that we won't serve Him in calamity. So, God has a motive in the suffering, but that does not make Him the Creator of the calamity.

But doesn't God plan some deaths for the purpose of making something good happen?

In 1529, in the town of Alzey (southwest of present-day Mainz, Germany) the state church authorities jailed nine true Christian believers. To make sure the revival ended, the court sentenced the men to be killed by the sword, and the women to be drowned in a pond. But the killings had the opposite effect.

> In this way the persecutors tried to put out the light of truth, but it burned more and more brightly. They took prisoner woman or man, servant or young girl—anyone who had embraced the faith and left the world and its idolatrous ways. In some places the prisons were full of them. This was done in an attempt to intimidate people. The prisoners responded

with such joyful singing that their enemies outside the prison became much more fearful than the prisoners inside. They did not know what to do with them, especially since they were imprisoned merely for the sake of their faith.

The count palatine then acted on the imperial mandate, and in a short time more than 350 brothers and sisters were executed because of their faith. In particular Dietrich von Schonberg, the burgrave of Alzey, had many believers in that town beheaded or drowned. . . . Not one recanted; they met death with joy. While brothers or sisters were being executed or drowned, those who were waiting sang until the executioner took them too. They were all steadfast and firm in the faith they had received from God. . . .

The burgrave of Alzey himself said, "What shall I do? The more I condemn and execute, the more of them there are."[3]

Does the fact that persecution can cause people to come to God mean that God causes persecution to save people?

When a youth dies, and the next week three of his friends are saved, does that mean that God took the youth's life to save his friends? When a failing father loses his child in an accident, and then recommits his life to God, does that mean that God took the child for the purpose of saving the father?

The Bible does not indicate that because someone is saved after the death of a loved one, or because someone becomes spiritually stronger after a death, that God caused the death for the purpose of bringing good.

In spite of it

What the Bible does indicate is this: Satan has the power of death. But when he gives his ultimate strike, God can and does accomplish good *in spite of* it.

---

3. *The Chronicle of the Hutterian Brethren, Volume 1* (Ste. Agathe, Manitoba: Plough Publishing House, 1987) pp. 74, 75. Used by permission.

In spite of it? Yes. When someone is saved after a death, that is God's power to accomplish good *in spite of* what the dog of death has done.

The sovereignty of God does not mean that He does everything that happens. His sovereignty is much more amazing and strong than that. He is so strong that He can allow angels and men to choose to fall, yet in spite of what they do, He can spoil "principalities and powers." He makes "a shew of them openly, triumphing over them in it."[4]

But didn't God cause Christ's death?

Peter says that Christ as a lamb "was foreordained before the foundation of the world, but was manifest in these last times for you."[5] John says Jesus was "the Lamb slain from the foundation of the world."[6] Jesus was delivered to His murderers "by the determinate counsel and foreknowledge of God."[7]

The Trinity agreed before the Creation that the soul that sins would die. They also agreed that the Son would give His life so that sinners would have an opportunity to be saved.

God knew that Christ the man would die. He also knew how Christ would die. But the Bible does not say that God caused the death of His Son or that God killed His Son. In fact, the Bible expressly says that Satan and wicked men caused the death of Christ and that *they* murdered Him.

> But we speak the wisdom of God in a mystery, even the hidden wisdom, which God ordained before the world unto

---

4. Colossians 2:15
5. 1 Peter 1:19, 20. See also Luke 12:22.
6. Revelation 13:8
7. Acts 2:23

> our glory: Which none of the princes of this world knew: for had they known it, they would not have crucified the Lord of glory (1 Corinthians 2:7, 8).
>
> Him . . . have ye taken, and by wicked hands have crucified and slain (Acts 2:23).
>
> But ye denied the Holy One and Just . . . and killed the Prince of life (Acts 3:14, 15).
>
> . . . they have slain them which shewed before of the coming of the Just One; of whom ye have been now the betrayers and murderers (Acts 7:52).

God planned that Christ would save man from sin, but He did not plan sin. God did not make a world where man had to sin. He did not make a world where man had to die. He did not make a world where there had to be a Redeemer. But He knew that man would sin, so He made a plan whereby people could be saved from their own choice to serve sin and Satan.

Now we are back to Steve Saint's question, "If God could plan the death of His own righteous Son, why couldn't He plan the death of my dad?"

Merle Ruth answers as follows.

> According to God's purpose, Jesus died in a foreordained way and at a foreordained time. Repeatedly, Jesus spoke of His approaching hour. Unlike the death of Jesus, your death and mine will likely come about by what we might call natural processes. . . . The idea that God engineers every experience that comes into one's life, including the time and manner of his death, is without Biblical support.[8]

When death is a result of disease, aging, accidents, and persecution—all results of the Fall—we have no authority to say that a death was God's will or God's plan.

---

8. Merle Ruth, "Correcting a Faulty View of Divine Providence," *The Eastern Mennonite Testimony*, January 2008, p. 5.

People often use a sequence of events surrounding a death as logical evidence that God must have planned the event. However, there is an alternate view that I believe is more true to the Bible. For example, in the Saint case—

- Satan caused the murder of the five missionaries to keep the Aucas firmly in his grip and to make Christians afraid and discouraged.
- Far beyond Satan's ability to comprehend, the Spirit of God began to move among the Aucas and gave them the opportunity to hear His Word.
- Far, far beyond Satan's ability to comprehend, the deaths inspired a greater love for truth and deeper loyalty to God in thousands of Christians, many of whom went on to share the Gospel in a way they never had before.
- God did not need to cause Nate Saint's death in order to win. In a far greater show of sovereignty, He accomplished His aims in spite of what the devil did.
- In fact, the "wisdom of God in a mystery" is so great that He can take Satan's very actions and utilize them to resoundingly defeat the kingdom of darkness.
- Our God is much greater than the sort of God who would have to plan and cause evil to accomplish good.

The foundation we need to survive

Even when we understand that God does not *make* tragedies, we still wrestle with why He *allows* tragedies.

The Bible answers that question by teaching us that the devil is the original source of all tragedy. The world today is not as God created it, nor as He desires it to be. God did not choose a world of tragedy, man did.

In response to man's tragic choice, God offered a plan of redemption. Christ's death opened the way to eternal life, where for God's children all tragedy will be gloriously healed forever.

While that does not answer all of the questions that face us in personal tragedy, it does give us the foundation we need to survive until we leave this world.

- We are relieved of accepting tragedy and death as part of God's good design. They are not.

- Being a faithful Christian does not mean that we are happy about death and that we need to say we wouldn't have life any other way. God isn't happy about death, and He would rather have the world another way.

- We can rejoice in spite of tragedy. God does!

- We can be at peace in spite of death. God is!

Study Questions

1. Study Job 1:10-21. In what way was Job in the power of Satan? What was God's involvement in the taking away of Job's belongings and family?

2. How is our God much greater than the sort of God who would have to plan and cause evil to accomplish good?

3. Discuss some examples of how God has utilized Satan's activities to defeat Satan's agenda.

4. List Bible verses that give us a foundation for survival until we leave this world.

15

"God Placed That Van in the Path of That Truck"

Does God plan accidents?

Rounding a curve on a snowy Pennsylvania road, Susan felt her van slide. Momentarily, she brought the vehicle under control. But a few seconds later her tires lost traction on the icy pavement, and her van slid in front of a loaded grain truck in the oncoming lane. She and her three-year-old son Melvin died in the accident, leaving my brother and his surviving children bereft of wife, mother, son, and brother.

A young friend of their family, no doubt struggling with the enormous loss himself, assured one of my bereaved nephews that "God placed that van in front of that truck." Many people have come to similar conclusions. Poems such as the following are common in sympathy letters.

> Things don't just happen to those who love God;
>> They are planned by His own dear hand;
> Then molded and shaped and timed by His clock.
>> Things don't just happen—they're planned.

> Things don't just happen to the children of God,
>> The blueprint was made by His hand,
> He designed all the details to conform to His Son,
>> So all things that happen are planned.

No doubt, the writers of these lines thought that they were helping grieving people to cope with their losses. As Merle Ruth writes, people "somehow feel that what we commonly call an accident is easier to bear if we view it as a divine appointment."[1] And so some comforters go so far as to say that there are no accidents with God.

No accidents with God? An accident is an unintentional event. If God intended everything that happens, there are no accidents. "Don't ever forget," said one man to another after an automobile accident, "that this accident happened exactly the way that God planned it."

Such a statement conflicts with itself. If everything was planned, the concept of accidents or even the word *accident* would not exist. But the concept of accidents does exist, because unintended events happen. God told us that unintended events would happen, and the history of the world proves what He said.

---

1. Ruth, *Correcting*, p. 4.

God told us that accidents will occur.

Exodus 21 and 22 are full of *ifs*—things that could happen, but that neither God nor man planned to make happen. *If* men were fighting and accidentally hurt an expectant mother . . . *If* a man blinded his servant or knocked his tooth out . . . *If* an ox gored someone to death . . . *If* someone left an uncovered hole, and an animal fell into it and died . . . *If* someone was caring for his friend's livestock, and the animal accidentally died or was hurt. . . .

Deuteronomy 19:4 and 5 describe death that happens without intention, such as when an ax head flies from its handle. Deuteronomy 22:8 commands the Israelites to build walls around their flat roofs to keep people from accidentally falling. The same chapter says what to do when a bird's nest "chance to be before thee."

In 1 Samuel 6:9, the Philistines did an experiment to see whether God was punishing them or if "it was a chance that happened unto us." In 2 Samuel 1, a young man "happened by chance upon Mount Gilboa," where Saul asked him to end his life. "It came to pass" as five-year-old Mephibosheth's nurse fled, that the boy fell and permanently damaged his feet. Ecclesiastes 9 declares that "time and chance happeneth to them all." Finally, in Luke 10, Jesus Christ Himself says that "by chance there came down a certain priest" who saw a poor wounded traveler, but passed by on the other side.

There are ifs. There are unintended events. Some things happen by chance.

God taught us safety measures because He does not stop every enraged bull. He does not suspend the law of gravity every time He sees someone about to fall from a roof. He knows the fallen state of bulls and men, and He knows the fallen nature of the natural world. He expects that fallenness to produce some injuries and deaths.

If God Himself expects accidents to happen among fallen mankind, how could we claim that everything that occurs is God's intention?

My brother's keeper

Since the Fall, tigers occasionally eat men. Deer and moose collide with cars. Vehicle brakes fail and hydraulic cylinders malfunction. Workers sometimes forget to disconnect electrical devices before servicing them. Drivers become drowsy and hurt themselves and others in vehicle wrecks. God does not deal with these things by saying "There are no accidents with Me. I made the tiger eat the man. I burst your brake fluid line. I tore the cylinder packing. I made the electrician forget to power down the device. I made the driver in the oncoming lane go to sleep and collide with you."

Instead, He urges us to be responsible and careful because by taking safety precautions, we can often keep accidents from occurring. Safety is important to God and important to His people. In fact, God built that truth into humanity so securely that even people who do not believe in Him still practice and teach safety. They call it a moral obligation, and a moral obligation it is.

When God asked Cain, "Where is Abel thy brother?," Cain asked defensively, "Am I my brother's keeper?" Cain was responsible to keep Abel as safe as possible. You and I have the same obligation to our fellow men.

No one picnics happily by the lake while a drowning person cries from the water. The picnic is forgotten; the crisis demands total attention. Involuntarily, people give the problem every ounce of their strength. Why is that? It is because accidents are not God's will, and He has morally obligated us to do all in our power to save life.

If accidents were God's will, there would be no need for emergency services, no moral obligation to rescue people in danger, and no responsibility to keep our brother.

People are responsible for accidents.

The Old Testament justice system, as well as modern laws, are built around the fact that people, not God, are responsible for the errors that result in accidents.

In the Old Testament God established cities of refuge to protect a person who accidentally hurt or killed another. He did not establish cities of refuge to deal with accidents that He caused, but with accidents that people caused.

Mankind is also responsible for the fact that accidents are in the world. There were no accidents in Eden; they came into the world along with sin. We are no longer as alert and wise as we were before the Fall. We err in judgment. We become old, weak, and tired.

Furthermore, we are bound with thousands of other people who also become old, weak, and tired. Accidents can happen to us when other people err or do wrong. God does not necessarily shield us from the results of what other people do.

We cannot assign the responsibility for our fallenness and our failures to God. Accidents came into the world because man disobeyed God.

Don't tempt God.

How many times has God intervened in His natural laws and kept us safe in an accident or kept us from an accident? Nobody knows. We praise God for the times that a miracle saved us, yet we do not run unnecessary risks, hoping for a miracle to see us through. When Satan tempted Christ to jump from a pinnacle of the temple and trust God to keep Him safe, Christ replied, "Thou shalt not tempt the Lord thy God."[2] By that example, Christ taught us that expecting God to intervene and save us from the effects of breaking natural law is foolish. God wants us to use common sense.

Angels watch over us, and they save us many times. But they are doing God's bidding, not our bidding. We cannot force their hand. God does not necessarily shield anyone, Christian or not, from His inexorable laws that govern the universe.

If we want to live out our seventy years, we need to live in harmony with the laws that God built into the world. If we come up against these laws, they will not break, but you and I will.

God established natural laws to help us avoid accidents, not to cause accidents. God does not want us to take unnecessary risks, because the outcome might be an accident.

"My boy was a good boy; why did God let it happen?"

Leslie Parrot tells the tragic story of four faithful Christian young men from Washington who suffered a severe accident. One evening they traveled several hours to a young people's meeting, using one of their fathers' cars. After the meeting, they had a meal, then started for home.

---

2   Matthew 4:5-7

One of them said, "I don't get sleepy while I'm driving, so you all go to sleep and I will drive you home." At 2:30 AM, on Interstate 5 between Portland and Seattle, the driver fell asleep. At seventy-five miles per hour, the car slammed into a concrete bridge pillar. Pieces of the car were scattered along a quarter-mile of the highway. Two of the boys were dead; the lives of the other two hung by a thread.

At dawn Leslie went to tell the parents of one of the dead boys about the accident. He told the boy's mother, and she went into shock. All she could do was walk back and forth, repeating, "My boy was a good boy, why did God let it happen?"

If you hit a bridge at seventy-five miles per hour, you will pay the penalty whether you are a good boy or a bad boy. God has laws that govern what happens when two tons of flying steel slam into one hundred tons of immobile concrete. The fact that God has established those laws does not mean that He is responsible for the results when we ignore them.

This is true whether we cause an accident ourselves or whether others cause us to have an accident. In 2019 in Minneapolis, a criminal entered a multi-story mall, grabbed a young child, and threw him over a low wall into the open center of the building. The boy fell several floors and was critically injured.

Did God want to injure that little boy? Of course not! The criminal was defying God when he threw the boy over the wall. But the innocent boy suffered nevertheless. When his body hit the concrete, he paid the price regardless of the fact that he was innocent. The fact that God did not stop the law of gravity for the lad falling in the mall does not mean that He wanted him to be injured.

God's laws also apply to our physical and mental health. If we pay too little attention to the laws that govern our bodies and minds, we will pay the penalty. To presume on God's mercy for physical and mental health while ignoring His laws is folly. God gives people divine strength to fulfill His calling, but this strength is given so that Christians may obey His voice, not so they may ignore His laws.

No one is exempt from God's laws. If we ignore them we will pay the penalty.

"If that is true, I can't even move!"

Several years ago, I was riding with my brother-in-law while we discussed whether God plans every detail of our lives. We came to a town as we talked, and stopped at a traffic light. The light turned green, but he didn't drive ahead. "If what you are saying is true," he declared, "I'm afraid to move! My life is in my hands. I can't even pull away from this intersection."

Yes and no. It is a risk to pull away from a stop light, but it is also a risk to stay there! There is risk in being born; there is risk in being alive. We are at risk because we live in fallen bodies, among fallen people, in a fallen world where a fallen angel prowls.

But no, we do not have to be afraid to get out of bed, eat food, drive cars, and live normal life. God watches over us and hears our prayers. He gives us His comforting Spirit and guardian angels. He performs miracles for us, and will finally take us to a risk-free eternity.

"Thou compassest my path and my lying down."

Psalm 139 is a wonderful base on which to move confidently through a risk-filled world.

In this psalm, God tells us that we have responsibility. We have our thoughts, our ways, and our path. We get up, we sit down, and we lay down. Even when we do these things in the fear of God, we nevertheless choose how to do them among many options that God blesses. We might choose a house from many options, decide which car to drive among many good choices, choose a church among those faithful to God, or decide who to marry among a number of fine Christians. Sometimes these choices work well, and sometimes they do not. God helps us make these choices, nevertheless they are our choices. They are risky choices because our own fallenness and the fallenness of other people will affect how our decisions play out.

Yes, our lives are in our hands and in the hands of our fellowmen, but our lives are also in God's hands. The cause and effect of human choice is involved, and so is the sovereign control of Almighty God.

While Psalm 139 mentions our responsibilities, it focuses on the fact that God is with us in this risk-filled world. In spite of the fact that we rejected Him, He did not leave this planet to spin off into oblivion. He made a way for us to come back to Him. He wants to be with us; He *is* with us. That is real comfort.

Our God is so merciful, so wise, and so present, that we can live without even thinking much about risk. Our God is so kind and so forgiving that He gives an eternal home even to Christians who make tragic or fatal mistakes because of their fallen bodies. That is real comfort.

Our God gives His full attention to each of us, and often directs His angels to our rescue, both physical and spiritual. His eye watches us better than we watch ourselves, and infinitely better than anyone else can watch us! That is real comfort, much greater than the comfort derived from the idea that God is causing every misfortune.

Meditate on this psalm.

> O Lord, thou hast searched me, and known me. Thou knowest my downsitting and mine uprising, thou understandest my thought afar off. Thou compassest my path and my lying down, and art acquainted with all my ways. . . .
>
> Thou hast beset me behind and before, and laid thine hand upon me. Such knowledge is too wonderful for me; it is high, I cannot attain unto it. Whither shall I go from thy spirit? or whither shall I flee from thy presence? If I ascend up into heaven, thou art there: if I make my bed in hell, behold, thou art there. If I take the wings of the morning, and dwell in the uttermost parts of the sea; Even there shall thy hand lead me, and thy right hand shall hold me. . . . Yea, the darkness hideth not from thee; but the night shineth as the day: the darkness and the light are both alike to Thee (Psalm 139:1-3; 5-10; 12).

Drive on! The light is green. "For whether we live, we live unto the Lord; and whether we die, we die unto the Lord: whether we live therefore, or die, we are the Lord's" (Romans 14:8).

"For God hath not appointed us to wrath, but to obtain salvation by our Lord Jesus Christ, Who died for us, that, whether we wake or sleep, we should live together with him" (1 Thessalonians 5:9, 10). What comfort!

Now, let's consider several other questions about accidents.

Does the fact that God does something good through an accident mean that He caused it?

God is able to take even the worst experiences that the Fall brings into our lives and use them for His glory. Through such experiences, He can draw us closer to Him, lead a sinner to salvation, or revive a person who was leaving Him.

The fact that God does something good as a result of an accident does not mean that He caused it for that purpose, but that He is so great that He can accomplish good in spite of the errors of fallen man and the evil of the devil.

Does God ever use something that seems like an accident to judge sin?

Yes, He does. When He does that, the happening is not an accident, although it might appear like one to onlookers.

When God took the wheels off the Egyptians' war chariots, it was no accident.[3] When "a certain man drew a bow at a venture, and smote the king of Israel between the joints of the harness," it was no accident. God had warned Ahab that he would die if he went into this battle. In one more defiant act against the God he had always defied, Ahab went into battle anyway, and there he died.[4]

When Absalom swung by his head, tangled in an oak, it was no accident. The God who said "the wicked shall fall by his own wickedness"[5] caused this evil man to reap what he sowed.[6]

In *An Asian Harvest*, Paul Hattaway tells the story of a revival in several Buddhist villages in Myanmar. When the Buddhist monks heard about these new Christians, they hired two gangs of thugs to beat up the new believers with chains and machetes, burn their houses, and violate the women.

One of the gangs traveled to the Christian villages by foot. As they walked through a mountain pass, a thunderstorm raged, and the entire group was killed by lightning.

---

3. Exodus 14
4. 2 Chronicles 18
5. Proverbs 11:5
6. 2 Samuel 18

The other gang boarded a raft and headed downriver to the Christian villages. A thick fog descended, and the raft collided with a barge. The thugs were thrown overboard and perished in the river.[7] In the context, such happenings were likely divine justice.

If God does not plan accidents, why do some people have a premonition of danger or death?

Kiyoshi Watanabe was a Japanese minister in a Japanese military prison camp in World War II. He followed Christ's command to love his enemies, and he often risked his life to help British prisoners with food, medicine, and other needs. His wife and most of his family were at home in Hiroshima, and as the war went on, Kiyoshi felt a sense of impending doom. One night early in August 1945 he felt especially depressed, and despaired of ever seeing his wife again. He wept without restraint into his pillow, and spent hours praying for his wife and two daughters in Hiroshima. For some reason, he prayed that they would be able to get away from the city. But hours later, a bomb called "Little Boy" dropped from the underbelly of an airplane, and fell toward Hiroshima. Kiyoshi Watanabe never again saw his wife and daughters on this earth.

Why did Kiyoshi Watanabe feel this premonition?

Premonition is a mystery. God reveals things to us through His Spirit, and this may include divine knowledge of spiritual battles and impending attacks from the evil one. However, that God knows about spiritual battles and impending evil attacks does not make Him the planner and causer of such events.

---

7. (Grand Rapids, MI: Monarch Books, 2017) p. 263.

I do not know what spiritual battles occurred before my son Winston died, but certainly there were battles. Soon after he was born, I would hold him each morning as I read God's Word. Over and over I thought, "This is too good to be true. This can't last." My wife was puzzled because I often mentioned that having a son was so wonderful; how could it last?

A short time before his accidental death, I paused one day with my hand on our bedroom door and asked Brenda, "What if something happens to Winston?"

She looked up, surprised. "You mean—when he's older?" With one hand she caressed the golden brown curls of our son in her arms.

"Maybe," I said slowly. "I don't know . . ."

Premonition is a call to prayer. When you feel a burden to pray for a friend, pray! God is speaking to you. When Lot was in danger of losing his life in the destruction of Sodom, God asked Himself, "Shall I hide from Abraham that thing which I do?" He told Abraham about it, and Abraham pled desperately for the righteous souls in Sodom. Because of that pleading, God saved Lot.[8]

Some dangers that threaten us come directly from Satan's schemes. When Satan wanted to prove that he could make Job curse God, he asked God for permission to test Job, and God granted it. An epic battle loomed, and the spiritual world was all attention. Would God win or would Satan win in this war for Job's soul?

When there is war for the soul of your child, your brother, or your neighbor, God is looking for someone to pray and to care! Your intercession may lead God to save someone from

8. Genesis 18:17; 19:29.

danger, or perhaps it will give a Christian courage in spite of an accident. Best of all, it may bring a soul to salvation, as it did for Lot.[9]

If we are oversensitive and fearful, prayer will help us give our premonitions and fears to God and go on with courage, whether we live or die. Whatever Satan and the Fall brings to us, whatever God allows us to suffer, we say with Paul,

> So now also Christ shall be magnified in my body, whether it be by life, or by death. For to me to live is Christ, and to die is gain (Philippians 1:20, 21).

Now *that* is real comfort.

Study Questions

1. Why would the concept of an accident not exist if God intended everything that happens?

2. Why would civil law and justice be impossible if God caused the errors that result in accidents?

3. Give some examples of wise safety practices in everyday life.

4. What happens when we ignore God's natural laws?

5. How can we live confidently and serenely in a risk-filled world?

---

9. 2 Peter 2:7

16

"Healing All That Were Oppressed of the Devil"

Does God make sickness, disease, and deformity?

In the 1600s, disease decimated the Native Americans in New England. So many people died that there was no way for the living to bury them. At times, English settlers found silent villages with skulls and skeletons lying on the floors of collapsed native houses. Why did it happen? God wanted the Puritans to overtake the region, said the Puritan preachers.

In 1918 and 1919, the Spanish flu took the lives of over 25 million people worldwide. Pastors around the world stated that the flu was a divine judgment on sin.

Why does a sweet saint lie suffering for years? Why does an innocent first-grader develop an inoperable tumor and die before his helpless parents' eyes? Why does sickness and disease happen to toddlers, even to babies before they are born? Does God make all this happen?

Sigmund Freud, the famous Austrian psychoanalyst, said that there is no God. But if there is one, he declared, he was going to stand before Him someday and hold up the cancerous bones of a little child and say, "Why?"

As a Christian girl mulled over these problems, she came to the conclusion that God is responsible for sickness.

> I remember the night I fought this out with God. I knew well what I needed to do, but I did not want to do it. . . . Finally I did it. "Thank You, Lord, for allowing three of my friends to battle with depression. Thank You that Carolyn's mom died of cancer. Thank You that Stephanie's daughter is epileptic. . . . Thanks for giving me stomach flu. I don't know why, and I don't know what's good about it, and I don't even want to say this, but You win. Thank You."[1]

But is God responsible for these things? Does He win by making poor sick mortals admit that He gave them stomach flu and that it is good? What does the Bible say about sickness?

God can make people sick.

When the Egyptians refused to release the Israelites from slavery, God sent terrible boils to man and beast. The Lord "smote Nabal," an evil man who refused to be courteous to David, by something akin to a heart attack or severe stroke.

---

1. "Of Thanksgiving and Stomach Flu," *The King's Daughter*, Fall 2016, p. 4.

When King David sinned in adultery and gave "great occasion to the enemies of the Lord to blaspheme," the Lord struck the illegitimate baby with sickness, and the baby died.[2]

When Gehazi lied to receive riches, he was covered with leprosy. The Lord sent a fatal disease to Jeroboam, the man infamous for making Israel sin. Jehoram did "evil in the eyes of the LORD," and "the LORD smote him in his bowels with an incurable disease."[3]

In Deuteronomy 28, God lists curse after curse that He would send on people who refused to obey Him, such as scabs and itches, blindness, and mental derangement.

As discussed in Chapter 11, when people follow the devil, God sees to it that they get the devil's rewards. That may include disease and sickness. But the fact that God can make people sick does not mean that He created sickness.

In the Old Testament, God told the Israelites to expect random sickness and pain.

God told the Israelites that anyone who was deformed, blind, blemished, or scabbed could not be a priest. God expected disease and deformity to occur randomly among them. He also told them what to do when and if sickness occurred, because sickness and spreading infections were not His will.

Over and over the Bible repeats the concept of random sickness. "When a man shall have in the skin of his flesh a rising, a scab, or a bright spot . . ." "If . . . the scab spreadeth in the skin . . ." "if a leprosy break out abroad in the skin . . ." "If a man or woman have a plague . . ." "When any man hath a running issue out of his flesh . . ."

---

2. Exodus 9:10, 11; 1 Samuel 25:37, 38; 2 Samuel 12:14-18
3. 2 Kings 5:27; 2 Chronicles 13:20; 2 Chronicles 21:5-20

Several times in the Old Testament, God promised that He would remove sickness and disease from the Israelites if they would serve Him.[4] Both of these references specifically mention the plagues of Egypt. These references seem to mean that God would not plague His people if they served Him. They obviously do not mean that no godly person would ever be sick, because the Old Testament tells of innocent and godly people who became sick.

Jesus Christ willed healing, not sickness.

When a leper came to Christ and said "Lord, if thou wilt, thou canst make me clean," did Jesus tell him, "If you have leprosy, that is God's will for you"? No, Jesus said to him, "I will; be thou clean."

When a centurion of Capernaum asked Jesus to heal his palsy-afflicted servant, did Jesus say, "The palsy is God's will for your servant?" No, He healed the servant the same hour.

The same theme is repeated dozens of times in the Gospels. Jesus healed people to show that He was the Son of God. Those miracles demonstrate that sickness and death is not His will.

Jesus tells us that sickness is not necessarily a sign that the sufferer has sinned.

"And as Jesus passed by, he saw a man which was blind from his birth. And his disciples asked him, saying, Master, who did sin, this man, or his parents, that he was born blind?

Jesus answered, Neither hath this man sinned, nor his parents: but that the works of God should be made manifest in him (John 9:1-3).

Even a sickness that is not God's will is an opportunity for the "works of God" to be demonstrated.

---

4. Exodus 15:26; Deuteronomy 7:15

The Bible tells us that sickness is a result of Satan's work in the world.

Luke 13 tells of a woman who was "bowed together, and could in no wise lift up herself." Jesus said, "Ought not this woman, being a daughter of Abraham, whom Satan hath bound, lo, these eighteen years, be loosed from this bond on the sabbath day?" Who was the source of this woman's deformity? Satan!

In Acts 10, Peter testified that Jesus "went about doing good, and healing all that were oppressed of the devil; for God was with him." What did Jesus heal? The work of the devil!

In 2 Corinthians 12, Paul said "There was given to me a thorn in the flesh, the messenger of Satan to buffet me, lest I should be exalted above measure." Where did Paul's infirmity come from? Satan!

So does Satan personally plan all of my sicknesses?

The Bible does not indicate that Satan is personally involved in all sickness. In fact, it often describes sickness just like we do. "In those days was Hezekiah sick to the death." Peter's mother-in-law was "sick of a fever." "And it came to pass, that the father of Publius lay sick of a fever and of a bloody flux . . ."[5]

We say the same things today. "I had a cold last week." "Did you hear that Paul has cancer?" "Beth's baby is sick with a fever."

While all sickness comes from the devil's work, the devil is not omnipresent, omnipotent, or omniscient. Instead of every sickness being a result of the devil personally touching you, it is more accurate to view our illnesses as a result of the corruption that Satan began—corruption that will make us sick time after time. Germs and infections will circulate until time ends.

---

5. 2 Chronicles 32:24; Matthew 8:14; Acts 28:8

If your child gets chicken pox, it generally means that she was exposed to someone who had chicken pox in the contagious stage. It does not usually mean that Satan personally infected your child with chicken pox.

However, remember that Satan personally smote Job with boils from head to foot. Satan has the power to do such things when God allows him to do so, as the following story shows.

My father-in-law traveled to Nigeria numerous times for church work. Once, as he walked to church, there was a strange object lying on the sidewalk. "Don't touch that thing," warned several of his friends. "It has a curse on it."

But one young man paid no attention to the warning. He kicked the object off the sidewalk, and the next day he was in bed with a severely infected leg.

Satan has a limited power over our physical bodies. Don't mock that power, but on the other hand, don't become preoccupied with it. "Fear not them which kill the body," Jesus said, "but are not able to kill the soul."[6]

The fact that mankind can control or even eliminate some sickness proves that in general, sickness happens by chance—"time and chance happeneth to them all" (Ecclesiastes 9:11).

Healthy diets, hygiene, medicines, and vaccines reduce life-threatening illness and result in longer average lifespans. Many diseases, such as whooping cough and polio, no longer pose the threat they once did, because of vaccines.

Smallpox killed over 300 million people in the 1900s. But God blessed the efforts to eliminate that disease by vaccination.

---

6. Matthew 10:28

The last known case of smallpox was in 1977. By 1980, smallpox was eradicated, and smallpox vaccination throughout the world ceased. The only known smallpox viruses today are confined in laboratories. (To date, smallpox is the only disease which mankind has apparently eradicated.)

If God had eternally planned for people to get smallpox, they would have gotten smallpox, vaccinated or not. The truth is that the Fall caused the corruption that brought smallpox, and God gave man the opportunity to eradicate it by applying life-saving health principles. God did not simply choose that smallpox would afflict man until 1977, then eradicate it by divine decree. God gave man the choice to use His principles to overcome smallpox. Had mankind ignored that opportunity, we would still be afflicted by smallpox.

You can reduce the number of times you get the common cold simply by washing your hands well. You can avoid scurvy by getting enough vitamin C. You can reduce headaches by drinking enough water and getting enough rest. Obviously, some aspects of our health are up to us. We can take advantage of God's revealed processes of health, or we can ignore them.

The fact that we can reduce our incidences of sickness and even eradicate a disease like smallpox shows that most sickness is neither God's personal plan for us nor the devil's personal scheme against us. Much sickness simply happens by chance contact with germs, overexposure to contaminants, the fallen genes that we have inherited, or by pushing our bodies past their natural limits.

God would not have revealed ways of battling sickness if sickness was His very good Creation. The miracles of surgery and medicine would not exist if sickness in general was God's will. In fact, how our bodies can build immunity and heal are ways that God's good Creation resists the effects of the Fall.

However, while we can avoid some sickness, we cannot avoid all of it. Satan corrupted the world, and this corrupted world afflicts us, no matter how well we wash our hands.

When you are sick, remember Paul's teaching.

Since the Fall, we are tempted to take pride in our health, our strength, and our looks. Paul testified that infirmity and weakness, though it came from Satan, helped to keep him humble. It does the same for us.

Some people turn against God in sickness, but others turn to God in times of sickness. That is what happened with Paul. Satan designed Paul's "thorn in the flesh"[7] for an evil purpose, and God allowed Paul to experience it. Paul prayed for release from the thorn, but God replied, "My grace is sufficient for thee: for my strength is made perfect in weakness."

"Most gladly therefore will I rather glory in my infirmities," Paul decided, "that the power of Christ may rest upon me." He wanted Christ's power at any price. He determined that in his life, Christ would triumph over the devil, regardless of the pain of the thorn.

Sickness is a messenger from Satan. In sickness, God does not tell us, "this thorn is my perfect gift to you." Instead He says, "My grace is sufficient for thee." So don't cry, "You win! Thank you for this thorn!" Don't blame God for Satan's work.

Instead, praise God for His sovereign ability to turn circumstances intended for despondency and defeat into opportunities to display His marvelous grace and power.

7. 2 Corinthians 12:7

God didn't make corruption. He didn't plan evil. He didn't design sin. He made GRACE! He made STRENGTH!

God didn't make disease. He didn't plan starvation. He didn't design asphyxiation. He made ETERNAL LIFE!

That is real comfort, much greater than the idea that God creates sickness for you because He sees that it is exactly what you need.

Study Questions

1. Why is it inconsistent with the Scriptures to believe that God sends all sickness and that it is good?

2. Jesus could have proved His divinity in many ways. Suggest some reasons why He primarily used miracles of healing.

3. Why has God revealed medical procedures and healing methods to mankind?

4. If we walk with God in times of sickness, how might the experience benefit us?

17

"It is Good For Me That I Have Been Afflicted"

Does God cause sickness to teach us lessons?

The Bible says "For our light affliction, which is but for a moment, worketh for us a far more exceeding and eternal weight of glory . . . for the things which are seen are temporal; but the things which are not seen are eternal" (2 Corinthians 4:17, 18).

Christians learn lessons in sickness. But the Bible does not portray God as designing sickness to teach His children lessons. Instead, it shows that God teaches us and strengthens us in the very experiences the devil designed for our downfall. The psalmist observed, "Before I was afflicted I went astray, but now have I kept thy word. . . . It is good for me that I have been afflicted; that I might learn thy statutes."[1]

Many people interpret such verses to say that affliction is good. But this verse does not say that. It says, "It is good for me that I have been afflicted." This is an important distinction.

Allow me to explain.

In the first verses of Romans 5, Paul declares that we are justified by faith and rejoicing in the glory of God. Because of that, he says, we glory in tribulations, "knowing that tribulation worketh patience." Does this mean that tribulation is good and is God's perfect design for us?

All tribulation is a result of the Fall and subsequent sin. We don't glory in tribulation because tribulation is good. We glory in tribulation because *God* is good. We glory in tribulation because God can, in our suffering because of the Fall, multiply our patience, experience, and hope.

God doesn't love tribulation, and we don't either. God does not praise tribulation, and we don't either. We praise the glory and grace of God, and we *endure* tribulation. God is also enduring this time of sin, tribulation, and fallenness, until He stops it. Endure with Him! But do not call the effects of sin and the Fall *good*, because He does not do that.

Times without number, God has turned the devil's design into an opportunity for His kingdom to advance. Does that mean that God made the devil's design? No. Does that mean affliction is good? No. But it does mean that God does good things *in the midst of* affliction. When we respond to Him in faith, He makes good things happen in bad times.

---

1. Psalm 119:67, 71

But the Bible says, "Who maketh the dumb, or deaf, or the seeing or the blind? have not I the LORD?"

> "And Moses said unto the LORD, O my LORD, I am not eloquent, neither heretofore, nor since thou hast spoken unto thy servant: but I am slow of speech, and of a slow tongue.
>
> "And the LORD said unto him, Who hath made man's mouth? or who maketh the dumb, or deaf, or the seeing, or the blind? have not I the Lord?" (Exodus 4:10-11).

In this passage, God reassures the handicapped that He created them, but He does not say that He created dumbness, deafness, and blindness. In essence, God is telling Moses, "I created you and I can help you do My will, no matter what is wrong with you."

God created us, and the Fall corrupted and damaged us. Even babies in the womb suffer from that damage, through no fault of their own. The damage they bear is not God's perfect design.

God can heal disability with a single word. However, many times He waits until eternity to do so. In this life, He usually lets us suffer the physical results of man's choice to sin, but gives us spiritual power to rise above our disabilities. He does not simply stand by watching us suffer, but gives us grace greater than our trial.

But the Bible says that "the LORD had shut up"[2] Hannah's womb.

For some reason, God did not let Hannah bear children at that time. Another such instance occurred when Abimelech took Abraham's wife, Sarah. In vengeance, the Lord "fast closed up all the wombs of the house of Abimelech." When Abimelech

---

2. 1 Samuel 1:5

returned Sarah to Abraham, "God healed Abimelech, and his wife, and his maidservants; and they bare children."[3] God can control fertility.

However, in most cases the Bible mentions infertility like any other abnormality.

- "But Sarai was barren; she had no child" (Genesis 11:30).
- "And Isaac intreated the Lord for [Rebekah], because she was barren" (Genesis 25:21).
- "But Rachel was barren" (Genesis 29:31).
- "Whose name was Manoah; and his wife was barren" (Judges 13:2).
- The great woman of Shunem "hath no child" (2 Kings 4:14).
- "And they had no child, because that Elisabeth was barren," (Luke 1:7).

The Bible also mentions the Lord healing childlessness at times. While God gives life, infertility is generally caused by the problems of the Fall. In the Scriptures, barrenness is not ascribed to God's will in the majority of cases.

Obviously, God does not withhold children because He is displeased with the lives of the people involved. If God did that, no child would ever be born from fornication or adultery.

Christian couples who struggle with infertility need not assume that God is displeased with them or does not want them to have children. They can pray for healing and yet recognize that God does not heal all the Fall's problems in this life. In many cases, they can adopt children or care for needy children. Thus, a situation that the devil meant for discouragement and bitterness can accomplish God's purposes in a hurting world.

---

3. Genesis 20:17, 18

But the Bible says, "He hath made everything beautiful in his time" (Ecclesiastes 3:11).

A young crippled girl, confined to a wheelchair for life, told her mother one day that she wished God would have given her the ability to walk. Her mother responded, "God loves you as much as He loves everyone else. The Bible says, 'He hath made everything beautiful.' Everything God made is exactly how He wants it. He makes no mistakes."

But Ecclesiastes 3 does not mean that everything in the world is beautiful, nor that everything is exactly as God wants it. Everything and every being in the world is fallen except God and the holy angels. In context, Ecclesiastes 3:11 simply means what Ecclesiastes 3 teaches: that there is a natural order and a natural time for things.

Of course God makes no mistakes. But fallen angels and people do. And what they have done has profoundly affected the world. Innocent little girls sit in wheelchairs all their lives because God's Creation has been spoiled by Satan's pride and mankind's choice. When those crippled little girls get to heaven, where "there will be no more curse,"[4] God will heal them.

If they were perfect on earth, He wouldn't have anything to heal. If there were no curse here, He wouldn't have any curse to remove.

Real comfort

Perhaps you or someone you love is diseased or handicapped and you take comfort in the thought that God specifically planned this disease or handicap—that it is His perfect will. I do not want to destroy your comfort; but I want to lead you to a greater comfort.

4. Revelation 22:2, 3

Remember Jesus' story of the beggar Lazarus in Luke 16? Lazarus was godly man. He spent his days lying on the street at a rich man's gate, and the only apparent care he received was that the street dogs licked his sores. Did Jesus say that Lazarus' disease was God's will for him? Did He say that God had planned Lazarus' pain to teach him (or someone else) lessons, and therefore his affliction was good?

Not at all. Jesus stated that in life Lazarus received "evil things"—bad things, things that made God sad. Lazarus was godly, and he still suffered.

God pitied Lazarus as a father pities his children. God knew Lazarus' frame; He remembered that he was dust. And God sustained him until He called him home to eternal life. Jesus' story illustrates that regardless of what the Fall brings to your physical life, God will sustain your soul and you can choose to triumph in Christ eternally.

The beautiful thing about God's grace is not that He plans handicaps and then calls them perfect. The beauty of His grace is that *in spite of* handicaps and all other problems of this fallen world, God is more than able to help you lie on the street in rags and running sores for His glory. He is able to heal you for His glory, to be sick for His glory, or even to die for His glory.

When sick or deformed people bear fruit for God, they are a great witness of God's grace in the human spirit. Such Christians inspire countless others to greater faithfulness, not because God deformed them, but because God saved them. They inspire others, not because what they experienced was God's plan or the best thing for them, but because they seized amazing grace in the face of overwhelming pain!

Like Lazarus, we may receive evil things in life. That matters, but not for long. One day soon, all disease and handicaps will be gone. The leaves of the tree of life are for our healing, and they cannot fail.

In Psalm 41:3, David says that when a godly man is in trouble, "The LORD will strengthen him upon the bed of languishing: thou wilt make all his bed in his sickness." Perhaps you remember times that you were sick as a child, and how your mother tucked you into bed and showed you special attentions. God strengthens you and makes your bed in sickness.

That is real comfort.

Study Questions

1. What is the right way to glory in tribulation?

2. What can we learn about sickness from the story of Lazarus in Luke 16?

3. Give examples or stories of suffering Christians who inspired others through their faithfulness in trial.

18

Of Tires, Trials, and Thieves

Does God plan every circumstance of my life?

M ike, if you knew that tire leaked, why didn't you take it off and fix it?" Fred Keller shouted. "That tire is almost new, and it's worth two hundred dollars. If you keep forgetting and you keep driving, you are going to ruin it! Don't say, 'I forgot.' When you know a tire leaks, take it off and repair it!"

Is it really my fault if I ruin my tire? Why can't I just say, "It was supposed to be, or it wouldn't have happened?"

Why not say, "Everything that happens is in God's plan. He is weaving me like a tapestry, and today that means a blown tire!"

Does God cause my thoughtlessness and carelessness? If my cookies burn because I am reading a book and forgot to take them out of the oven, did God burn my cookies? If I accidentally leave open the pasture gate and my cows cause a wreck on the highway, is that God's doing?

No! God has given us common sense and the responsibility to act on it. We chide ourselves for our mistakes because we did not use the common sense and free will that God gave us to the best advantage.

Certainly, God can make me forget something if He wishes to do so. But when my fallenness has caused problems, should I comfort myself with, "God's way is best, I will not murmur?" That would be great fantasy, not great faith. God didn't cause the problems; *I* did.

The Bible teaches that we have some free will to cause and change circumstances. If we accept that, we cannot say, "this is God's will" the moment things go wrong.

But what about circumstances that are beyond our power to control? Doesn't God cause them?

Certainly, He causes some of them. You and I did not choose to have Jesus Christ sent to the world, but here He is to save us. You and I did not create the beauty of the world, but here it is for us to enjoy. You and I did not create the mystery of childbirth, the marvel of human friendship, the joy of marriage, the miracle of forgiveness, or the security of a faithful church. But here they are, enriching our lives! Who made these blessings? God did.

But there are other circumstances that Satan brings into our lives, as he brought them into Job's life. Apostle Paul tried several times to go to Thessalonica to encourage the believers, but he didn't succeed because Satan hindered him.[1] As long as we live in the world, we will be affected by poor circumstances that the devil, the Fall, other people, and we ourselves cause.

This is the same world the New Testament church lived in—and they faced tribulation, distress, persecution, famine, nakedness, peril, and sword. Paul did not say that God willed these things. To the contrary, he said that the reason they faced these things was because of angels, principalities, powers, and creatures whose aim is to separate Christians from God's love. Read Romans 8:31-39.

Many things happen to us beyond our power to control, but that does not mean God is causing them. Instead, God is making sure that nothing can separate us from His love.

Because of our fallen nature and the fallen nature of our fellow men, there is no way to guarantee that everything in our life will turn out well.

In *God of the Possible*,[2] Gregory Boyd tells the story of a young woman whose faith was nearly shattered because of the fallen circumstances Satan brought into her life.

Suzanne was raised in a godly home and gave her life to Christ as a young girl. As a young woman, she felt that God was calling her to be a missionary in Taiwan. So she prayed that God would lead her to a young Christian man who was totally dedicated to God, also had a burden for Taiwan, and would be committed to raising a godly family.

Eventually, Suzanne met a young man who shared her ideals and goals. They courted for over three years, prayed

---

1. 1 Thessalonians 2:18
2. (Baker Books, Grand Rapids, Mi.: 2000).

together, and attended church together. Even after that extensive courtship, when the man proposed to marry Suzanne, she did not immediately say yes. She wanted to be sure that he was the right one.

To find God's will, both of them prayed and fasted numerous times for the next several months. They sought advice from their Christian parents and other friends, all of whom agreed that this marriage was the Lord's will. Eventually, Suzanne had the assurance she sought, and she married him.

Within two years after their marriage, however, Suzanne's husband was involved in adultery. At first he repented, but he continued to fail over the next several years. His Christian life died, and their marriage steadily decayed. He fought with Suzanne verbally and even struck her physically, once breaking her cheekbone. Eventually he filed for divorce and moved in with another woman.

The awful ordeal left Suzanne emotionally and spiritually bankrupt. Besides feeling like her life was basically over, she lost her spiritual zeal and struggled to maintain her belief in God. She could not understand how the Lord could answer her life-long prayers by leading her to marry a man who would fail so utterly. She had had such clear confirmation that she should marry him, and it seemed to her that if God had not led her to do it, then no one could ever be sure that God was leading them in anything.

Some of her friends suggested that God had indeed led her to this man, for the specific purpose of teaching her lessons through his sin and rejection. In other words, God saw she *needed* this affliction, and though it was a terrible trial, it was "all for the best."

Eventually Suzanne realized that Satan and her husband, not God, had brought about the sad circumstances in her life. God *had* led her to marry her husband. When she did, her husband was a godly man, the kind that God wanted her to marry. The failure in her marriage did not mean that she had rebelled against God in marrying her husband. The fact that God taught her in these circumstances did not mean that He caused the circumstances to teach her a lesson, nor that a failed marriage was the best thing that could happen to her.

Many sincere Christians have wondered, "How can I be sure that the person I marry (or the one my child will marry) will be faithful to God for life? How can I know that this union will not cause me grief?" It is impossible for you and me to guarantee that our lives will turn out the way we want them to. We cannot even guarantee that our circumstances will turn out the way *God* wants them to, because sin has entered the world. God Himself does not force everything to turn out the way He wants it.

However, we have the promise that in the end, for His faithful followers, God will restore all things and wipe away our tears. We have the guarantee that the new heaven and earth will be worth everything we have experienced. That is real comfort.

Poor circumstances do not indicate that God is displeased with us.

> There were present at that season some that told him of the Galilaeans, whose blood Pilate had mingled with their sacrifices. And Jesus answering said unto them, Suppose ye that these Galilaeans were sinners above all the Galilaeans, because they suffered such things? I tell you, Nay: but, except ye repent, ye shall all likewise perish.

Or those eighteen, upon whom the tower of Siloam fell, and slew them, think ye that they were sinners above all men that dwelt in Jerusalem? I tell you, Nay: but, except ye repent, ye shall all likewise perish (Luke 13:1-5).

In Hebrews 11, some believers had amazing circumstances. They subdued kingdoms and obtained promises. Their dead came to life and they turned their enemies to flight. Do those descriptions make you wonder if you are truly a Christian? Maybe nothing like that seems to happen for you.

Notice, though, the two little words *and others* in verse 35. Here the circumstances change. These people were tortured and killed; mocked and beaten. They had no homes, and little clothing and food. They wandered in the wilderness taking shelter in dens and caves.

Was there something wrong with them? Was God treating them this way because they needed special lessons? No. They were people of deep faith, and the world was not worthy of them. To God they were all heroes of faith, regardless of their circumstances. That is still true today. If you are a child of God, you are a hero of faith, regardless of your circumstances.

Your relationship to God is determined by your faithfulness, not by your circumstances.

But is it safe to live if God does not plan all of my circumstances?

Maybe this is a scary thought. But life would be even more scary if God did plan all the problems and evils that happen.

Suppose that a gang has been going around your community stealing things and terrorizing residents. You know that you could be the next victim, so you take precautions. You lock your doors and repair your yard light. You pull your car keys and put your things away.

But if you believe that God plans all your circumstances, taking precautions is contradictory. If God is instigating the thieves to hit you next, and directing them what to take, there is nothing you *can* do about it. And if He is keeping them from hitting you, there is nothing you *need* to do about it. Either way, there is nothing for you to do.

If you take precautions, you do not believe God has ordained the thieves' next move. If you pull keys and lock doors, you believe you may be able to alter what happens.

My dad always said that he locked his doors and pulled his car keys to keep honest men honest. He believed that what he did could alter circumstances that otherwise might come to pass.

So why would life be even more scary if God planned all the problems and evil that happens to everyone? If God is the kind of God that ordains such evils, then you can't trust His character. You have nothing to hold onto in this evil world if God is like that. For all you know, He might be planning that your car will be stolen. Far worse, He might be planning to turn you into a car thief!

How ridiculous. Thank God, He is true to His character. The world is still scary, but far less so than if we had a God whose character permitted Him to ordain every circumstance that we face.

Real comfort

The comfort of thinking that God does everything is far surpassed by the comfort of knowing God as the Bible describes Him. This God has chosen not to control all circumstances, yet He often works behind the scenes in circumstances for His glory and our good. This God has chosen not to stop all evil, yet He often works miracles to protect us from danger. This God gives us common sense, yet because mankind has chosen to fall, He lets us choose our way and face the law of sowing and reaping.

God's arm is mighty to save us from the Fall He did not cause. His Word gives us the prudence to steer away from the foolishness He did not make. His Spirit teaches us and comforts us in all circumstances, even the ones He wishes would never have happened. And come what may from evil principalities and powers, if we but follow Him He has promised us a home in heaven. What more could we ask?

Study Questions

1. Why should we not claim, "This is God's will" the moment things go wrong?

2. List some circumstances that God has caused.

3. Why can't we guarantee that everything in our life will turn out well?

4. Describe aspects of God's character and promises that comfort us in difficult circumstances.

19

"All Things Work Together For Good"

A study of Romans 8:28 and similar Scriptures

R omans 8:28 says "And we know that all things work together for good to them that love God, to them who are the called according to his purpose." Does that mean that God plans all of our circumstances, and that they are good?

In *The Christian's Secret of a Happy Life*, Hannah Smith gives the classic reasoning developed from Romans 8:28.

> It may be the sin of man that originates the action, and therefore the thing itself cannot be said to be the will of God; but by the time it reaches us it has become God's will for us, and

must be accepted as directly from His hands. . . . If God be for us, it matters not who may be against us; nothing can disturb or harm us, except He shall see that it is best for us, and shall stand aside to let it pass.[1]

In short, because we love God, nothing can happen to us but what He wants to happen, and therefore all that happens to us is directly from His hands and is best for us.

I believe that Romans 8:28 is one of the most misused verses of our time. Allow me to explain.

Interpreting Scripture within its context is extremely important. The context of Romans 8:28 is how Christ frees us from condemnation, fills us with His Spirit, adopts us, gives us hope of heaven, sustains us in our infirmities, and intercedes with God for us.

I believe Romans 8:28 means that the things Paul describes in Romans 8—salvation, the Holy Spirit, adoption, heaven, and Christ's sustenance and intercession—all work together for good to them that love God.

"Wait a minute," you might say, "Romans 8:28 says *all things*. That means *everything*, right?"

Let's see how this interpretation would fit some other Scriptures that use the words "all things."

Paul states in Romans 14:20, "All things are pure." Does that mean everything is pure? No, in context that simply means that no physical food will harm you spiritually.

Paul says in 1 Corinthians 3:21, "All things are yours." Does this mean we may help ourselves to anything we see? No, in context Paul is explaining that the Christian possesses everything of eternal value.

---

1. (Grand Rapids, Mi.: Fleming H. Revell, 1952), pp. 148-157.

Is it lawful for us to do anything we want to do? Paul explains in 1 Corinthians 6:12, "All things are lawful unto me." No, in context this means that Paul's rights were the same as any other man's, but he would not insist on his rights in any way that offended others.

Should charity quietly bear sin in the church, believe lies, and hope for an opportunity to repent after death? Paul says in 1 Corinthians 13:7 that charity "beareth all things, believeth all things, hopeth all things." No, we understand these "all things" in the context of other Bible teachings.

Should we give thanks for sin? Paul says in Ephesians 5:20 that we should thank God "always for all things." No, in context Paul tells us to walk carefully and to thank God for His gifts.

> The Bible very clearly says that we can accomplish anything we want through Jesus. We can triumph in a beauty pageant, swim the English Channel, or crush an opponent in a boxing match. We can do all this because the Bible promises, "I can do all things through Christ who strengthens me" (Phil. 4:13).
>
> Not exactly. In context, Paul is teaching the Philippians about contentment (see verse 11). He can persevere through difficult times because Jesus gives him strength. In Philippians 4:13, we learn that Christ will give us power to accomplish the work He has commanded us to do.[2]

What would we have to believe if Romans 8:28 meant "*everything that exists* works together for good to them that love God"? We would have to believe that sin is good for us. We would have to believe that Satan works for our good. We would have to believe that victims of abuse are victims of God's will. But according to the Bible, those are false conclusions.

---

2. "The Three C's of Interpretation," *The Heartbeat of the Remnant*, Fall 2019, p. 7.

To believe that Romans 8:28 means that everything that happens is for our good is to fall prey to what Aden Gingerich calls the fragmentary method of Bible interpretation.

> This is a wrong method of interpretation because it is unethical and does injustice to the Scriptures. It does not take into consideration other parts of the context or the tenor of Scriptures, thus we miss the true meaning. This method is often applied to promises of God. . . . For example, Romans 8:28 in the context of the whole chapter gives us a different understanding than simply going to that one verse to prove that rain, snow, accidents, sickness, arthritis, or any happenings are all for our good. . . . in context all the provisions of adoption, hope, and the work of the Spirit are the "things" that "work together" for the good of the believers.[3]

Christians who have not personally been brought face-to-face with the heartrending reality of Satan's war against God are especially tempted to use Romans 8:28 out of context.

Interpreting the Scriptures according to their context is one of the main keys to "rightly dividing the word of truth."[4] False doctrine generally begins by using God's Word out of context. Satan tempted Christ to do that in Matthew 4, but the Son of God promptly replied with a godly use of Scripture.

We should understand Romans 8:28 in context, just as we understand all other Scriptures. Romans 8:28 is consistent with all other Scriptures when it is understood in context. [5]

---

3. "Rules for Bible Interpretation and Understanding," *The Christian Contender*, September 1993, p. 11.
4. 2 Timothy 4:15
5. In Romans 8:28, the NIV adds the word *in*: "And we know that *in* all things God works . . ." I believe this is still discussing the subjects of Romans 8. However, it could also mean that God works *in* all circumstances for the good of His children (other Scriptures agree with this). Nevertheless, it does not mean that God *plans* and *causes* all of our circumstances and calls them *good*.

But Joseph said "God did send me" to Egypt, and that "God meant it unto good." Doesn't that mean that God planned Joseph's abduction?

Joseph's remarks must be understood by all of the principles of God's Word.

To betray and sell Joseph was evil. This sin against God and Joseph weighed heavily on the brothers' consciences until they repented and were forgiven. God held it against them, and the brothers knew it. Acts 7:9 says that the brothers were "moved with envy." They were moved by the father of envy, Satan.

If the brothers had obeyed God and loved Joseph, God could have cared for Jacob and his family in some other way. It was not necessary for the brothers to sin in order to accomplish God's will. Everything that occurs against God's will should not have happened and does not need to happen.

Notice the order in which Joseph's story happened. In Genesis 45, Joseph tells his brothers twice that they sold him into Egypt. Then, he twice repeats that God sent him before them to preserve life.

Many theologians insist that both of these things happened simultaneously. In other words, God, using Joseph's brothers, caused a sin, carried out an abduction, and delivered Jacob's family through it all. In the end, everyone understands why God did what He did.

This storyline is often used to explain happenings. For example, it is sometimes stated that a woman's first husband died because God was arranging circumstances so her second husband could also enjoy marriage instead of being single for life.

According to the principles of God's Word, I submit an alternate view, using the Biblical order of events.

1. Joseph's brothers abducted him against God's voice in their conscience and in disrespect and disregard for their godly father. Satan inspired them to do it.

2. In the midst of the brothers' sin, God protected Joseph and positioned him so that the devil would not triumph in this evil circumstance. Instead of letting Joseph go off into oblivion, God sent him to Egypt and put him in Potiphar's care.

3. Because Joseph chose to be faithful to God, God had a righteous man in the exact spot he was needed to save Jacob's family. (Indeed, Joseph's faithfulness became God's tool to save the population of that whole region. The famine was "over all the face of the earth," and "all countries came into Egypt to Joseph for to buy corn.")

4. In the end, in spite of the brothers' sins and Satan's plan to wreck the righteous seed and vex the world through famine, God marvelously provided for Joseph, his family, and many others. Joseph even became a type of Christ—not because God planned and caused every circumstance of his life, but because God triumphed in the situation in spite of the devil.

Keep in mind that God's foreknowledge of an event does not make Him the planner or causer of any evil in the event.

Joseph didn't say "God caused my affliction." But he did say, "God hath caused me to be fruitful in the land of my affliction." There is a difference.

So, "God did send me" and "God meant it for good" does not mean that God planned and caused the evil in this story. Instead, these phrases describe God getting involved in the midst of sin and tragedy. In spite of the sin, God received glory. Because Joseph was faithful in tragedy, God was able to give the world this inspiring story.

God is so effective at bringing good out of evil circumstances that it may look like He planned the entire event, evil and all. But such a God would be much weaker than our God. Our God is so capable and wise that in events that He does not want to happen, He can bring about things that He does want to happen.

Evil does not accomplish good. *God* accomplishes good. That is why we praise God for all good that happens in any event. At the same time, we recognize the devil as the ultimate father of all evil that happens in any event. This is completely compatible in the Biblical understanding of God.

But doesn't James 4 teach that God plans everything in our lives?

> Go to now, ye that say, To day or to morrow we will go into such a city, and continue there a year, and buy and sell, and get gain: Whereas ye know not what shall be on the morrow. For what is your life? It is even a vapour, that appeareth for a little time, and then vanisheth away.
>
> For that ye ought to say, If the Lord will, we shall live, and do this, or that.
>
> But now ye rejoice in your boastings: all such rejoicing is evil. Therefore to him that knoweth to do good, and doeth it not, to him it is sin (James 4:13-17).

I once heard this passage explained like this: The reason we say, "The Lord willing" when we plan things is because God's will could decree otherwise. If our plan lines up with God's plan, He will allow no evil thing to thwart the plan. If God wills otherwise, our plan fails, but God's plan stands, and we are glad about it because we want His way.

Such an explanation ignores the war of the ages between God and Satan. It means that if you try to mend a broken relationship but fail, it was not God's will to heal the relationship. It means that if you try to lead a soul to Christ, and do not succeed, it was not God's will to save that soul. It means that if you plan to bale hay, but cannot because you did not properly maintain your baler, it was not God's will for you to bale hay. But we know from the Scriptures that such scenarios are false. The Bible clearly explains that wills besides God's will have a bearing on earthly circumstances.

In this passage, James is not denying the possibility of human choice and the work of the devil. Instead, the context of his teaching is people who are not only boasting, but also are *exulting* in *evil* boasting. They are focusing on earthly gain and treasure with no thought for their eternal welfare or the fact that their life is as smoke.

Instead of living like that, James teaches, we ought to say, "I want the Lord's will." Our first thought in any circumstance ought to be, "What is God's will in this situation?"

When we say, "Lord willing, we'll go to Grandpas tomorrow," that does not mean that only the Lord's will can change our plans. The decisions and actions of any number of free agents, including the devil, could change our plans. It simply means that if a situation occurs in which it is obvious that we should do something other than go to Grandpas, we will do that other thing. The fact that it becomes obvious that we should do something else does not mean that God made our child sick, flooded the highway, created the traffic jam, or made our vehicle break down in order to keep us in line with His eternal plan that we do not go to Grandpas today.

The fact that we keep in mind that we want to do God's will does not mean that no other wills operate in the universe. The fact that God can arrange anything He wishes to does not mean that everything we see is His arrangement. The old saying, "Lord willin' and the crick don't rise" recognizes this.

Paul recognized that the will of God or the will of man could create circumstances. One day, he and his missionary team "assayed to go into Bithynia: but the Spirit suffered them not."[6] Another day, he really wanted Apollos to go to Corinth, "but his will was not at all to come at this time; but he will come when he shall have convenient time."[7]

Does anyone suppose that God made the sharp contention between Paul and Barnabas in Acts 15? Was God trying to make more missionary teams, and couldn't figure out a better way to do it than to make these leaders struggle? No, the problem was that "Barnabas determined" and Paul "thought not good." The wills of men, not the will of God, caused the contention. In the circumstance that arose, the will of God enabled the men to separate, to do His work, and to both be a blessing.[8]

To say "the Lord willing" is a commitment to do and to accept God's will in everything we face, not a commitment to believe that God plans and causes everything we face.

---

6. Acts 16:7
7. 1 Corinthians 16:12
8. Acts 15:36-41.

But doesn't God weave every thread of my life?

Some popular songs imply that everything that happens is in God's "master plan." They claim that God is weaving every thread of our lives. Following common error, these songs take Romans 8:28 out of context. They teach that everything we face is God's will, was supposed to happen, and is wise and kind.

It is simply false, according to the Bible, that God weaves every thread of our lives. Certainly, He weaves much of our life, and the closer we walk with Him the better He can weave us. However, the truth is that we weave some threads, other people weave some threads, and Satan weaves some threads.

True, God never makes mistakes. But people do.

True, God is always kind to His children. But Satan is not!

Does that mean, then, that you and I are hopeless, hapless victims of circumstances? Where is the God of all comfort? Let's find out in the next chapter.

Study Questions

1. Why is it important to understand the Scriptures in their context?

2. List aspects of Joseph's story that God obviously did not cause.

3. List aspects of Joseph's story that God obviously did cause.

4. Explain the meaning of "If the Lord will."

20

"God Remembered Abraham"

Trusting a God who can change circumstances

One night in a big city, a small, poorly-dressed girl arrived at a drug store just at closing time. She asked for a certain medicine for her sick mother. Irritated at the last-minute delay, the pharmacist reluctantly prepared it.

After the child had left, he made a horrible discovery. By mistake, he had given her a poisonous substance! The girl was already out of sight, and the man had no idea where she lived.

Cold sweat broke out on the pharmacist's forehead. For the first time in years, he prayed.

After a little while, he heard a knock on his locked door. There stood the child again. "Please, mister," she said, "I stumbled and fell, and broke the bottle. Could I have some more medicine?"

Greatly relieved, the pharmacist quickly prepared the correct medicine.[1]

There are happenings that are accidental, but I believe that the little girl's fall was providential. We can assume some sad details from the story—the extremity of a small child out at night in a big city, a poverty-stricken family, perhaps no father and husband to care for them, maybe an orphan on the street had the mother died. There is an irreligious or backslidden pharmacist, who for the first time in years desperately turned to God and received confirmation that He hears prayer.

Did God have a hand in the broken bottle? By all accounts, yes. "Thou art the helper of the fatherless," David testified. And God told the wayward Jews, "Call unto me, and I will answer thee."

Second Kings tells of the childless Shunammite woman who kindly provided room and board for the prophet Elisha. In reward, Elisha promised that God would send her a son. When the boy was a child, he became ill and died, and Elijah restored him to life. Later, famine afflicted the land of Shunem, and the Shunammite woman and her household moved to Philistia for seven years. When she returned home, others had taken her land and house.

As was customary in Israel, she went to the king to ask that this wrong be made right. The day that she came to the court for help, Gehazi, Elisha's servant, was telling the king stories about Elisha's miracles.

---

1. As told by Merle Ruth.

"It came to pass," 2 Kings 8:5 says, "as he was telling the king how he had restored a dead body to life, that, behold, the woman, whose son he had restored to life, cried to the king for her house and for her land. And Gehazi said, My lord, O king, this is the woman, and this is her son, whom Elisha restored to life."

Amazed, the king appointed an officer to restore the stolen property. Certainly God arranged her circumstances! "The eyes of the Lord are upon the righteous, and his ears are open unto their cry."[2]

Now consider another story, "God's Way Is Best."[3]

An elderly Christian couple arrived home from an extended trip. When they entered their house, their kitchen faucet was running, and the sink was overflowing. Their nearly new house was a wreck. The kitchen cabinets were warped, the hardwood floors were ruined, the furniture and walls were soaked. After turning off the water and surveying their house with growing dismay, the couple prayed about their problem.

"Lord," prayed Grandpa, "we are thankful that you have a plan for our lives. . . . Help us to remember that you have a purpose for this. . . ."

Grandma prayed, "Lord, why did our happy week have to end like this? . . . Why did we have to go to all that work to have it ruined like this? . . . Help me to be submissive to your plan for our lives . . ."

After thinking back to the events before they left on their trip, the couple realized that the water supply had been shut off when they left. Grandma had left the faucet open and the

---

2. Psalm 34:15
3. *The Christian Example*, January 5, 2020, p. 4.

sink drain plugged, so when the utility company turned on the water, their house eventually flooded.

Now, on what basis could we conclude that God made Grandma leave the faucet on? On what basis could we conclude that the situation was God's way, God's plan, or God's purpose? On what basis could we conclude, as Grandma did, that their happy week *had* to end like this, and that their house *had* to be ruined?

There is no evidence that God goes around making people leave their faucets on. But there is much evidence that because of the Fall, people are forgetful. And this, I believe, is the reason Grandma's house got flooded—*she forgot to turn the faucet off.*

If we believe that God causes all such mishaps, why isn't that what we tell our children when they make such mistakes? When your child floods the bathroom, you don't just tell them that this was the way the day had to go, that this was God's plan, and that God's way is best! No, you give them a lesson on personal responsibility. They hear that they are NEVER to leave the bathroom with the water running! Why? Because they are responsible!

Does the fact that Grandma forgot to turn her faucet off and ruined her house mean that God had nothing to do with the situation? No.

"Amazing grace, how sweet the sound"

Grandma (and all of us like her) take great comfort in the fact that the God who sees the falling sparrows also sees the open faucets, and He cares for us in the details of our lives.

God's love and kindness shone through Grandpa and Grandma as they turned to God for grace to bear their disappointment. It shone through Grandpa's daughter, who gave them a home while they couldn't live in their house. It shone through the willingness of their Christian friends to help them repair their house.

Amazing grace also shines through the parent who finds the flooded bathroom. She is patient; she helps clean up the mess; she still loves her child through it all.

However, the fact that God's grace shines through a situation does not mean that God caused or planned the situation.

Now, dig a little deeper.

A wise mother plans her day so that she and her toddlers can handle it. That is wise and good, but not really amazing. If God was limited to simply planning your life so that He and you together could handle it, that would be wise and good, but not really amazing.

If God's grace would only help you with things that God had planned to come into your life, how would He help you when you fall into sin? How would He help you when someone you love turns away from Him? He doesn't plan those things.

A truly amazing Sovereign

The truth is that God's grace is so infinite and sovereign that He can help you in *anything* that you bring on yourself because of the Fall or your own foolishness. He will be with you through *anything* that anyone's thoughtlessness or evil brings into your life. In fact, He is so powerful that He can enable you to be true to Him through *anything* that the devil brings into your life!

That is truly amazing sovereignty. You and I can try to wisely plan our lives, but even then we get in over our heads.

179

But God can allow the free will of man and the sinister free will of Satan, yet is more than adequate to deal with *anything* that those free wills do.

It doesn't necessarily take much power to accomplish your purpose when you are the only one working. It takes infinitely much more power to accomplish your purpose when someone completely against you is working.

God never gets in over His head. That is not because He forces every man and every spirit to do His will. Nor is it because He creates every circumstance. Instead, it is because He can out-maneuver every effect of the Fall, every capability of evil man, and every power of the fallen angels. In fact, He can deal with situations that had never come to His mind, as Jeremiah 19:5 illustrates. "They have built also the high places of Baal, to burn their sons with fire for burnt offerings unto Baal, which I commanded not, nor spake it, neither came it into my mind."[4]

That is an amazing sovereignty—much more amazing than a God who could simply handle everything that He planned Himself.

> Without surrendering His sovereignty, God obviously permits a great deal of human activity that is directly contrary to His holy will. Nevertheless, and this is marvelous, nothing that God permits can defeat His overarching purposes. A true view of the sovereignty of God sees Him as so "big" that He can succeed in spite of all the contrary things He allows.[5]

Praise God when He has done a miracle for you or when it seems obvious that He has arranged circumstances to bless your life. Praise Him because what we see and understand of

---

4. See also Jeremiah 7:31 and 32:35.
5. Personal letter from Merle Ruth, October 23, 2008. Used by permission.

Him is just the beginning of His unsearchable work. Praise Him for His mystery, praise Him for love, praise Him because He will triumph over all in the end.

Now, will this mysterious, powerful Sovereign do things for us merely because we love Him and ask Him? Can we touch His heart and move His will? Can we influence Him to change some circumstances? Yes.

"God remembered Abraham"

"And it came to pass, when God destroyed the cities of the plain, that God remembered Abraham, and sent Lot out of the midst of the overthrow, when he overthrew the cities in the which Lot dwelt" (Genesis 19:29).

God remembered Abraham, and that is why He saved Lot when Sodom burned. Don't ever forget that. As a Christian interceding for the salvation of souls, you have power with God. Do what Abraham did! Plead with God because of His character, His love, and His mercy.

To have power with God, we must be the kind of person Abraham was. Abraham was humble—he felt like dust and ashes before God. Abraham was obedient—God said, "For I know him, that he will command his children and his household after him, and they shall keep the way of the LORD."

Does God know you and me to be that kind of person? When He does, He will respond to our cries.

Persistent intercession will change the spiritual circumstances of our community and church. The Bible says, "The effectual fervent prayer of a righteous man availeth much." That means the fervent prayers of the righteous can change the circumstances. Just because we do not know what changed does not mean that nothing changed.

If God had eternally ordained all circumstances, our prayers would change nothing. But He did not! Instead, he eternally decreed that the prayers of the righteous would help to change the world.

Why does the Lord's Prayer say, "Thy will be done in earth, as it is in heaven?" Because we are to pray for God's will to be done, not accept everything as though His will was automatically being done.

In Matthew 24, Jesus instructed His followers to leave Jerusalem when certain signs took place. He said, "But pray ye that your flight be not in the winter, neither on the sabbath day." Possibly God did not plan the season and time that the Romans would plunder Jerusalem. That may have been up to others, and in essence, Christ simply told His disciples, "This is going to be a bad experience. Plead with the Father to make it easier to bear."

"For the eyes of the LORD run to and fro throughout the whole earth, to shew himself strong in behalf of them whose heart is perfect toward him" (2 Chronicles 16:9).

Peter says, "The eyes of the Lord are over the righteous, and his ears are open unto their prayers: but the face of the Lord is against them that do evil" (1 Peter 3:12).

God is against evildoers, but He is for His children. Just as a father pities his children, so the Lord pities those that fear Him. He will show Himself strong for His children. For them, He will change the circumstances!

Don't say "Whatever will be, will be." Don't treat God as an untouchable, unreachable Sovereign that solemnly marches on His way without considering His people. If we have that attitude, it is very probable that God's will won't be done.

Pleading with God not only moves Him, it changes us.

When we plead with God, we become acutely aware of His voice. When we plead with Him, we walk with Him. "The steps of a good man are ordered by the LORD," but He can only order them if we are utterly depending on Him.

This utter dependence on God does not ensure that bad things will not happen to us. Even when the Lord is ordering our steps, some things in our lives will not turn out the way we want them or the way God wants them. In fact, the very next verse after "The steps of a good man are ordered by the LORD" tells us that the good man will occasionally fall. It does not say that the Lord ordered the fall, but it does say "the LORD upholdeth him with his hand."[6]

However, utter dependence on God does ensure that no matter what happens, God will care for us and carry us to the end. Utter dependence on God will also move Him to perform miracles for us.

One of my friends (I'll call him Gerald), in one of the darkest days of his life, had such a miracle. A fifteen-year-old young man gave his heart to the Lord in the church where Gerald was pastor. The young man confessed that some time earlier, he had broken the law. The situation was reported to the police, who took the teenager into custody. Now, unless a judge would release the boy to his parents, that evening he would be sent several hours away to a juvenile detention center. It would be a terrible experience for him, but only a few hours remained until evening, and it seemed impossible that the legal system could respond fast enough to evade what was sure to come.

---

6. Psalm 37:23, 24

183

The situation pierced Gerald's very soul. He was alone that day, feeling very depressed, wrestling in prayer with God for his young brother in the Lord.

A pickup pulled into the yard, and Gerald went to the door to see who had come. An old cowboy, a casual acquaintance of his, walked up. He handed $200 to Gerald, and turned to go back to his truck. Finally Gerald found his voice.

"W-wait a minute," he stammered. "What is this for?"

"The Lord takes care of those that need to be taken care of," the cowboy replied. He got in his truck and drove away.

The message went straight to Gerald's heart. He drove to the young boy's home and told his parents, "An 'angel' just came and told me that the Lord is taking care of your boy." Late in the day, a judge released the boy to the custody of his parents.

"I didn't need the money, and I shouldn't have needed an old cowboy to give me such a simple message," Gerald reflected. "But I did need him, and the Lord knew it and sent him to my door."

I am convinced that the Lord does far more miracles for us than we realize. But we are so fallen that we need the times when we don't get a miracle, too. As Randy Alcorn has written, "Miracles must be the exception, not the rule. Otherwise, our choices would have no real consequences."

God has a beautiful way of doing miracles without letting us demand them. He has an amazing way of working in circumstances without becoming responsible for every detail of our lives. He has a mysterious way of responding to prayer without being manipulated by those who ask amiss.

Ask! Plead! Intercede! Trust God because He can arrange any circumstance He wishes to. Trust Him because He is able to work in any circumstance that people and the devil cause. Trust Him because in every circumstance, He will show us a way to respond that brings us one step closer to heaven.

There, we will finally be where God arranges all circumstances.

Study Questions

1. Why can no person who accepts responsibility for his actions believe that God causes all mishaps?

2. Why does God never get into situations over His head?

3. How can a person have power with God? Discuss the advantages and limitations of this concept.

4. Why must miracles be the exception, not the rule?

21

"The Whole Creation Groaneth and Travaileth in Pain"

A Biblical view of weather and natural disasters

At the first cry of "Water!" from the rushing crowd on the street, Sinar knew what was happening. A tsunami! He was sure of it. An earthquake as massive as the one they had just experienced meant that a gigantic wave had been unleashed in the ocean and was coming into the city. . . .

He could clearly see boats and ships coming in on the crest of the wave, being tossed about like so many pieces of driftwood. He saw how the water hit the buildings, the waves splashing high over the roofs before pouring into the streets and alleys. The main wave came straight toward him. As the force of the wave pushed water up the parallel streets, Sinar watched as it dashed sideways down the alleys from both directions, trapping helpless people in the middle.

It all happened so devastatingly fast. Before he was aware of it, the water had risen up the walls of his building. The cars and tin roofs being swept along by the water made the wave look like liquid trash, hurtling at breakneck speed and picking up anything in its path.

Sinar winced as he saw bodies flying through the air in the onslaught. The roaring, moaning, grinding monster was so noisy that only occasionally could he hear the screams of the victims. But he could see them. . . .

The receding water revealed far more than wreckage. Scattered throughout the surreal landscape were the bodies of men, women, and children, sprawled on the wreckage, half buried in the mud, or lying silently side-by-side. The area lay in ruins worse than any battle scene. The earthquake had begun the damage, but the tsunami had wreaked far greater havoc.[1]

On December 26, 2004, the city of Banda Aceh on the island of Sumatra, Indonesia lost 80,000 of its 425,000 citizens. The earthquake and resulting tsunami that killed these people also killed thousands of others in the countries surrounding the epicenter in the Indian Ocean.

God is the Creator and Sustainer of the natural world. Does that mean that He is the author of the violence of nature? When a tsunami rushes ashore, claiming the lives of thousands, did God cause it? When a volcanic mountain erupts and covers towns, wilderness, and farmland, was that God's will?

Floods, hurricanes, and tornadoes kill thousands of people and ruin billions of dollars worth of assets every year. Insurance

---

1. Harvey Yoder, *Tsunami!* (Berlin, Oh.: TGS International, 2006) pp. 61, 62, 64. Used by permission.

companies call these things "acts of God." Are they right? What kind of God would make that kind of world?

The truth is, God didn't make that kind of world. God created Eden perfectly safe and beautiful. The earth was watered by mist, not by pelting rain. There was no damaging wind, no floods, droughts, hail, or erosion. There were no natural disasters in Eden.

Man, through Satan's temptations, wrecked the earth. *Man* chose to bring sin into the world, which caused the curse and every element of danger and unpleasantness. "Cursed is the ground for *thy* sake," God told Adam.[2] God built the earth, and man wrecked it. Don't blame the Builder; it was the occupants who trashed their home.

Now, Paul says, "The whole creation groaneth and travaileth in pain together" (Romans 8:22). The original wording of this passage clearly teaches that the earth is now subject to vanity or futility. It is in bondage to corruption. All nature, the climate, and the uneasy interior of the earth groans. Everything earthly is broken—the people, the animals, the rocks, the dirt, the water, the elements. Even "the stars are not pure in his sight."[3] This earthly system is aging and perishing.[4] The Fall is causing a gradual deterioration of the entire natural world.

In spite of the Fall, God's system of climate and weather still plays a major role in making the earth a safe, sustainable home. "For he maketh his sun to rise on the evil and on the good, and sendeth rain on the just and on the unjust."[5]

---

2. Genesis 3:17, emphasis added.
3. Job 25:5
4. Psalm 102:26; Hebrews 1:11-12
5. Matthew 5:45

God has unlimited power over nature.

> And [the cloud] is turned round about by his counsels: that they may do whatsoever he commandeth them upon the face of the world in the earth. He causeth it to come, whether for correction, or for his land, or for mercy (Job 37:12, 13).

> He giveth snow like wool: he scattereth the hoarfrost like ashes. He casteth forth his ice like morsels: who can stand before his cold? He sendeth out his word, and melteth them: he causeth his wind to blow, and the waters flow (Psalm 147:16-18).

> Praise the LORD from the earth, ye dragons, and all deeps: Fire, and hail; snow, and vapour; stormy wind fulfilling his word (Psalm 148:7, 8).

As God sent plague after plague on the Egyptians to make them set their Israelite slaves free, the Egyptian magicians told Pharaoh, "This is the finger of God."

Who judged Sodom and Gomorrah with what reminds us of a volcanic blast? God did.

In Numbers 16, God judged Korah, Dathan, and Abiram for their rebellion against Moses. The earth opened and swallowed them up, and scarcely had the earth closed upon them when the Lord sent a fire and consumed two hundred fifty priests who had supported the rebellion.

When the Amorites fought the Gibeonites because they made a league with Israel, Joshua and Israel's army went to aid Gibeon. As they fought the Amorites, "the Lord cast down great stones from heaven upon them" and more died from the hail than by the sword. Joshua wanted more time to complete the battle, so he asked God to make the sun stand still. "So the sun stood still in the midst of heaven, and hasted not to go down about a whole day."[6] On another occasion, "the Philistines drew near to battle against Israel: but the Lord thundered with a great thunder on that day upon the Philistines, and discomfited them; and they were smitten before Israel."[7]

God shut the heavens and caused drought at times to bring His people back to Him. The Lord "sent out a great wind into the sea" to get Jonah's attention. The book of Revelation describes natural disasters that God uses to show His authority and provide wake-up calls for the sinful world.

However, if you have a damaging storm, that does not mean you are a sinner. If you have sunshine the next day, that does not mean that you are a saint. Every day over most of the world, saints and sinners alike experience God's kindness in the climate. "Nevertheless he left not himself without witness," Paul told the men of Lystra, "In that he did good, and gave us rain from heaven, and fruitful seasons, filling our hearts with food and gladness."[8] Jesus taught in Luke 13 that we should never assume that a disaster is God's judgment on specific people, unless God clearly reveals that.

Every force of nature is at God's disposal. But not all the violence of nature is punishment for sin. Nor does God cause all of the violence of nature. Much natural violence is simply a result of the Fall. The broken, cursed system cannot operate as safely as God designed it to do originally.

Satan has limited power over nature.

In the story of Job, Satan caused fire to burned up Job's sheep and their keepers. He sent a great wind that flattened a

6. Joshua 10:6-14
7. 1 Samuel 7:10
8. Acts 14:17

house in which Job's children were gathered, killing all of them. And that was just in one day in the life of one man.

The book of Revelation describes the power given to hell to cause famine.[9] It pictures Satan using his power over nature to convince people to worship him. Because of him, we all feel the effects of this broken earth. However, God in mercy limits the sorrows and disasters the devil can cause.

Man has limited power over nature.

God has given mankind the wisdom to harness the energy of the relentless wave, the invisible wind, and the tumbling river. However, man sometimes causes disasters as he uses the elements.

> At 9:15 A.M., just after the children had settled into their first lesson on the morning of 21 October 1966, a waste tip from a South Wales [coal mine] slid into the quiet mining community of Aberfan. Of all the heart-rending tragedies of that day, none was worse than the fate of the village junior school. The black slime slithered down the man-made hillside and oozed its way into the classrooms. Unable to escape, five teachers and 109 children died.

While reporting the tragedy, the British broadcaster asked a clergyman the inevitable question about God's involvement. "Well . . ." he answered, "I suppose we have to admit that this is one of those occasions when the Almighty made a mistake."[10]

Who made the mistake? God didn't pile up the waste tip in a precarious situation. *Man* made the mistake.

God generally does not suspend natural laws when people do foolish things. The disaster of the South Fork Dam, situated

---

9. Revelation 6:8
10. Brian H. Edwards, *Not By Chance*, (Hertfordshire, England: Evangelical Press, 1982), p. 14.

on the Conemaugh River above Johnstown, Pennsylvania, illustrates this. The earthfill dam was poorly maintained and there were warnings that it would not hold up through heavy flood conditions, but the authorities paid little attention. On May 31, 1889, heavy rains caused the dam to collapse, sending a 30-foot high wall of water downstream. Johnstown was a booming steel center built on the floodplain of the river, and that day nearly half of the city was swept away. Over 2,200 people lost their lives, and 1,600 homes were destroyed.

God didn't build South Fork Dam, and He didn't maintain South Fork Dam. God didn't build Johnstown on the floodplain, and He didn't prevent people from building on the floodplain. People created the situation. Their poor decisions caused the disaster.

Reflecting on the 1900 hurricane that took 6,000 lives in Galveston, Texas, a Methodist pastor said, "Much of so-called Providence is human improvidence." Galveston had been built on an unstable barrier island, an extremely vulnerable site.

People often cause floods, fires, landslides, and pollution simply by ignoring the principles of the universe.

Even when we try to follow natural laws, we sometimes err. Our designs can fail. At best, our engineering is flawed. God can save us from the results of our poor decisions, but He does not necessarily do so. He could override our failures and always control atomic reactors, but He does not.

Under God's law, there is a freedom in the universe for natural principles to operate.

Years ago, a young Christian couple on their wedding trip drove through the Columbia Gorge. Far above the highway, there was a rock perched precariously.

No one knows why that rock came loose as the couple motored down the canyon highway. Some said it was caused by a sonic boom. Others said it was the bulldozers at work in the canyon far below. Others said that God had planned it or that it was chance.

That rock plunged down across the mountainside and crashed right through the roof of that car. It hit the young man square on the head and killed him instantly. With considerable presence of mind the young bride grabbed the steering wheel and guided the car safely off the road, avoiding further tragedy. Why did it happen?[11]

There is a freedom in the universe. Tornados and hurricanes hit saints and sinners alike. So does rain and drought. So do rocks.

God allows natural laws the freedom to function, and He does not always perform miracles to keep people out of harm's way. The tower of Siloam fell on 18 men, and God didn't stop it.[12]

Keep in mind that God designed natural laws to help us avoid accidents, not to cause accidents. However, in this fallen world, God told us to expect accidents. Everywhere you look in this world, you see both form and freedom, structure and spontaneity. There are unintentional events. Some things happen by chance. Now and then, because of the law of gravity that keeps us safe most of the time, a rock falls on someone. This happens because of the earth's fallen freedoms, not by God's perfect design.

---

11. As told by Leslie Parrott.
12. Luke 13:4

God expects us to use common sense to protect ourselves from dangerous elements.

"Sirs, I perceive that this voyage will be with hurt and much damage," said Paul, "not only of the lading and ship, but also of our lives."

Paul was traveling under guard to Rome, but his ship could barely make headway in the contrary wind. Finally, the safe season for sailing was past. The storm season was beginning, and Paul knew it was too risky to go on.

But the crew and captain did not want to winter in Fair Haven, the Cretan town where they now lay at anchor. Phenice, only fifty miles to the west, was a much nicer place. So when a soft wind blew from the south, they disregarded Paul's advice, hoisted the anchor, and made for Phenice.

Soon after they left, a terrible storm drove them off course. For two weeks the storm pushed their ship west, and they finally shipwrecked on the island of Malta, some 300 miles from Phenice. Read the story in Acts 27.

In this story, notice Paul's beliefs about the weather. The season of storms was beginning, so he expected that it was dangerous to sail. He did not believe that whether or not their ship ran into a storm was simply ordained by God. He knew the weather patterns, and he believed that God did not want the ship and its crew to take unnecessary risks.

Even after their ship was storm-tossed for many days, Paul did not conclude that God had designed this storm to drive them to the place where He wanted them. Instead, he told the crew that they should have listened to him and remained in Fair Havens. If they would have, they would not be in such danger. However, he assured them, that though the ship would be lost, they would be saved.

That story summarizes a New Testament view of the weather. We should respect predictable weather systems. God's will is to avoid risk—in Paul's case, to preserve life and goods by wintering in an inconvenient harbor. God generally doesn't stop the patterns of nature just to save people from the results of foolish decisions.

Let's summarize.

- In the beginning, God made the climate and geology perfect. That is the way He wanted it.

- In the fall, the climate and geology were cursed. The Flood brought further degradation. The climate still sustains life, but it also became potentially dangerous and deadly.

- In spite of the curse, God did not abandon the earth. He exercises direct control over the weather whenever He chooses to do so. Even when He does not exercise direct control, the entire weather system is still regulated by His natural laws. God wants us to understand those laws in order to minimize danger and loss of life.

- God restrains and rules over the fallen conditions on the earth to keep it habitable. God has unlimited power over nature. "Thou rulest the raging of the sea," says Psalm 89:9, "when the waves thereof arise, thou stillest them." Nahum says, "The LORD hath his way in the whirlwind and in the storm, and the clouds are the dust of his feet" (1:3).

Pleasant, beautiful conditions and abundant harvests are all God's doing. All destructive, degrading, and dangerous conditions are because of the cursed earth or because of how fallen man uses the earth. The fact that God may use and direct dangerous conditions to warn and judge people does not mean that He wanted those conditions to be on the earth.

So there are two things operating together in the natural world—the will of God in giving us a life-sustaining climate, and the sin-caused brokenness of that system causing damage and havoc.

Because of that, it is right to praise God for rain, and it is right to sandbag rivers. It is right to recognize that the power of fire is from God, and right to recognize that in this fallen world, fire can be extremely dangerous.

When houses sweep down a swollen river, great faith does not solemnly insist that God willed us the perfect amount of rain. When a wildfire is burning a town, great faith does not declare that God lit the town. Instead, great faith is busy repairing and controlling the effects of the Fall. In rain or other natural events, we see both God's blessings *and* the stamp of the Fall.

God mercifully sustains us in this groaning world.

In spite of the Fall, weather patterns are fairly consistent, repeated, and predictable. This is God's mercy to us.

God has also given man the wisdom to predict and prepare for disasters, to build to withstand common disasters, and to identify and avoid highly dangerous areas. He mercifully helps us to cope with what sin has done to the once-perfect world. Furthermore, He often miraculously protects us from the fury of the elements.

In disaster, God reminds people that the world is coming to an end. In disaster, God uses Christians who are willing to aid others as a testimony of Christ's love. In disaster, God uses Christians who praise Him *in spite of* the world's fallenness, not *because of* it. In disaster, God hears our cry and pities and comforts us as a father pities and comforts his children.

Someday soon, God's children will live in a new heaven and a new earth, forever free from the fallen powers of nature on this earth. In that place, "there shall be no more curse: but the throne of God and of the Lamb shall be in it." There will be no disasters, tears, death, sorrow, or pain, "for the former things are passed away." "They shall hunger no more, neither thirst anymore; neither shall the sun light on them, nor any heat."[13]

Now *that* is real comfort—much greater than the comfort from the idea that all that happens in this groaning world is God's perfect plan.

Study Questions

1. Contrast Eden with the present groaning Creation.

2. List some principles of the natural world that are found in Scripture.

3. What are some evidences of God's tender care for us in this fallen world?

4. In what ways does God speak in disaster?

---

13. Revelation 22:3; 21:4; 7:16

22

But Why Me, Lord?

The question that won't go away

Why me? In essence, that is the question Moses asked when God wanted him to lead Israel out of Egypt, an assignment that changed his life completely. That is the question Job asked. That was the question on David's mind as he fled from King Saul. Jeremiah faced this question. Jesus Christ himself asked, "Why hast thou forsaken me?" Reduce that question to its minimum and it is "Why me?"

It is right to ask that question. When we cry "God, why me?" His loving heart is touched. He will come to us in compassion and grace and bind our wounds and help us to live for Him. When a groaning spirit cries "Why me?" in unspeakable anguish, the Son intercedes and the Father hears. Help will come!

The religious world has come up with many answers for "Why me?" Let's examine a few of them.

The religious world says that when you suffer, God is preparing you for greater things.

That is true, but not because you are suffering. It is true simply because, if you are God's child, God is preparing you for heaven every day of your life.

The world's emphasis is that when you are suffering, you should hold on because your moment of fame is just around the corner. You are about to be given a greater role in life.

This self-centered idea has no place in the Christian life. This is a cheap substitute for simply being faithful until death because you love the Lord Jesus Christ.

I know this is a hard truth. The fact is, we like to think that any setback now is somehow tied to inevitable success. You wanted to court that girl and she said no, so God must have someone much better lined up for you. You don't have much money now, but God must be refining you so you can handle large amounts later. You are carrying a lunch pail today— surely God is preparing you to manage employees in your own business down the road. You are putting up with a small house now—God is teaching you contentment so you will be able to appreciate a spacious home in the future.

What if you are single for life? What if you are poor all your life? What if you are never self-employed, never manage an employee, or never have a convenient house? Will that mean that God overlooked you or didn't care for you?

Do you know how most of the Old Testament prophets lived and died? In suffering and obscurity, with hardly any visible fruit for their life work.

We never read that after Herod killed their children, the bereaved Bethlehem mothers began a counseling and therapy center that helped thousands. Jesus healed a woman that had bled for twelve years, and one that was sick for eighteen years, and we never hear of them again. Jesus raised Lazarus from the dead, and as far as we know he lived an ordinary life until he died again.

Dorcas generously spent her days sewing clothing for widows and ragamuffins. All who knew her loved her. The result? She became sick and died, only to be brought back from the dead to do it again.

Abel worshipped God and was murdered for it. Jonathan gave up his natural right to kingship and supported God's call to David. After his life of unswerving loyalty to God, he was killed on Mount Gilboa along with Saul, just as if there was no difference between him and his self-crazed father. In obedience to God, Naboth wouldn't sell his vineyard to Ahab. At the end of the day, Ahab strolled in the vineyard and Naboth lay very, very still. John the Baptist introduced Jesus to the world, boldly preached against sin, and lost his head for it.

Many a faithful Christian has lived out his days forgotten and sick and helpless and never knew anything different until he woke on glory's shore. Many a saintly father and mother in a humble home have cried and prayed for their wayward children and died without seeing their prayers answered.

We suffer because of the fallen world. We suffer because of the epic struggle between Satan and God. That is the basic reason for all the suffering in the world.

Expect nothing but to suffer in obscurity with Jesus Christ. Strive for nothing but to suffer in a way that glorifies God. Aim for nothing but to suffer faithfully, that you might reign with Christ!

The world says that when you suffer, God is using your suffering to create a great story.

When I lived in the Philippines, I once was on our narrow village street when a drunk driver came toward me. Enraged that my jeep was in his way, he rammed his vehicle into mine several times. Somehow, I got out of his way, and he tore madly down the street.

An hour or two later, as my neighbors and I were talking about the incident, the drunk man crept up behind me and took me by the neck in the crook of his powerful arm. After a tense conversation, in which I apologized repeatedly for being in his way, the drunk raised the arm with which he held me, and with great force hurled a razor-sharp machete into the ground in front of us. Only then did I realize that the point of that machete had been at my throat throughout the conversation.

In a few days, I took some fresh pineapples from our field and visited my now-sober attacker. He was extremely nervous, but we had a nice conversation and put the incident behind us.

A few weeks later, my son Winston died. My attacker was among the neighbors that came to the wake. The same strong arm went around me and hugged me, while he whispered his sympathy for me.

When I told someone the story, he was elated. "You know what is going to happen?" he cried. "There is a third part to this story coming. I believe that drunk is going to come to Jesus Christ through Winston's death. There has to be a reason for this! Things like this don't just happen!"

Before long, we moved to another area, and I never saw the man again. I never heard that he was saved. I know of no one who came to Christ through Winston's death. (That does not mean that no one did.)

When you suffer, the general teaching of the Bible is that you are suffering because of the Fall, sin, and Satan, not that God is causing the suffering as part of a wonderful plot. No great story needs to come of your suffering; no marvelous chain of events needs to unfold.

When we have had a narrow escape or a close brush with death, we feel "shook up." In those moments we feel absolutely convinced that God must have saved us for a purpose. He has something for us to do; He has a reason for sparing us. This is true, but not generally because some great work awaits us. It is true simply because God has a work and purpose for every Christian every day as long as he lives.

This is another hard truth, but "Why me?" does not need a glamorous answer. Don't assume it has one. Don't look for it. Many people who imagine glamorous answers end up making themselves the sacrificing hero. But the story is already told, and Jesus Christ is the hero. You and I are merely obscure characters in the old, old story of God's triumph over Satan.

Don't confuse the results of suffering with the reason for suffering.

The *reason* for suffering is the devil. The *results* of suffering can be for God or for the devil, depending on what the sufferer chooses.

Satan's plot is sinister: to cause as many people as possible to suffer as much as possible. That is the plot in your suffering, and it is with evil intent.

God's salvation is wonderful: to bring as many as "call on the Lord" to grace and comfort now and to eternal life in the future. That is the reason He walks with us in suffering, and it can cause good in spite of an evil situation.

The key is humility: to understand that we are powerless in the grip of a sinister plot, but by humbly accepting God's salvation and sanctification, we can be lifted in the arms of grace.

The process is humiliating: over and over we realize and struggle with our helplessness, again and again we face the fact that in God alone—and eternity alone—will we be free from this corruption.

Until then, does God really care about obscure you and me, caught down here on earth in the gears of this cosmic battle? Yes, He does. And He answers when we cry "Why me?"

How did God answer Job?

A suffering Christian once told me that the book of Job made him angry. Job had a lot of good questions, and God didn't even answer them. Instead, He launched into a series of questions that Job could not answer, that had nothing to do with the subject of the conversation.

Or did they?

Job 40:8 helps us to understand this conversation. God asked Job, "Wilt thou also disannul my judgment? wilt thou condemn me, that thou mayest be righteous?" Job felt that he must be wrong, or God must be wrong. But in this verse, God told Job that he didn't need to condemn God in order to be righteous. In the reverse, neither did God condemn Job in order for Himself to be righteous. God tells us twice in the

204

book that Job was righteous, and even stated that Job had spoken of Him "the thing that is right."[1]

So, Job's problem was not that he was in the wrong or that he deserved this suffering. His problem was that he did not understand what was behind the scenes. He did not understand that the devil, not God, had caused his changing fortunes.

Now, back to why God asked Job so many questions instead of giving him the answers he longed for. Couldn't God have relieved Job by telling him what He told us? Maybe that *wouldn't* have relieved Job. Maybe it would have simply brought a new flood of questions. Apparently, what He did tell Job was more important for Job to know than what had taken place behind the scenes.

And what did He tell Job? In my words—

There are things in this situation that you do not know. Don't question my justice and love just because you do not know everything. I created and I sustain the entire natural world. Isn't that proof that I created you and will sustain you?

You don't need answers for all your questions. You need Me. The fact that I talk to you, love you, and will eventually right all wrongs is enough.

When you are suffering, remember what God told Job. That is more important than knowing the details of what is happening behind the scenes.

Remember, too, that every mortal in the book of Job thought that God's approval was shown in ease and prosperity, and that God's disapproval was shown in trouble and poverty. Satan used this false belief to his advantage.

---

1. Job 42:7

How did God answer John the Baptist?

John the Baptist, the faithful forerunner of Jesus Christ, was imprisoned for preaching the truth. Meanwhile, Jesus went on preaching to others, healing others, and working miracles for others. Some came to life, some were healed from the diseases that had bound them for years, and all who believed went away with a glad light in their eyes.

But John was locked away.

Why didn't Christ rescue him? Hadn't he been faithful to Jesus? Did Jesus think that somehow it was better if John was off the scene? Was there something wrong with the way he had taught about the coming Messiah? Questions burned in John's soul until the most basic question of all surfaced: *Was Jesus really the Messiah? The way this is turning out seems so wrong!*

Really, John! Your mother must have told you how the angel came to her, confirming that Mary, her cousin, was to be Jesus' mother. You leaped for joy before you were even born when Mary came to your mother's house. You must know the prophesies that your father spoke at your birth. You introduced Christ to your people, you baptized Him in the Jordan River. Didn't you hear the voice, "This is my beloved Son, in whom I am well pleased?"

Yes, John knew all that. But disappointment, discouragement, and tragedy can carry anyone to this point. Many of us have been torn by tragedy and carried down, down, down until we grappled with these very questions. *Are you really God? Are you really good?*

How did Jesus answer John's question? What reassurance would He send to that discouraged prisoner?

> "Go and shew John again those things which ye do hear and see: The blind receive their sight, and the lame walk, the

lepers are cleansed, and the deaf hear, the dead are raised up, and the poor shall have the gospel preached unto them."

"And blessed is he, whosoever shall not be offended in me" (Matthew 11:4-6).

We know from the Word of God that bad things happen because of the Fall, sin, and Satan. However, that truth will not answer all our questions in tragedy. God Himself does not answer all of our questions in tragedy. Evidently, answering those questions is not the most important thing. But from the stories of Job and John the Baptist, I believe God gives us truth to cling to when we feel deserted.

- I love you and will carry you in this hour. I sustain all the world, and I will sustain you. I am here, though you cannot see me.

- I will reward all righteousness and judge all evil. Be patient. Eternal, total deliverance is coming!

- The miracles you have witnessed, the spiritual victory you have experienced, and the life that you have lived in the Holy Spirit is as true as it ever was. Nothing has changed except that you are in overwhelming despair. I will never leave you or forsake you in your darkest hours.

- Though you cannot understand why I did not change your circumstances, do not be offended in Me. Do not charge Me with evil. Do not question my love for you because I am letting you suffer along with the rest of the groaning world. Let My glory shine through your broken, bleeding life. Do not be offended in Me!

"When he cried unto him, he heard"

Is there a God? If there is, is He good? Does He love us? What is faith?

My wife and I voiced those questions on sleepless nights after our son died. The heat of the tropics oppressed us. The curtains hung damp and lifeless in the breathless air. So our spirits drooped, suffocating. As the silent cell mocked John the Baptist, so the whine of mosquitos and the chirping lizards on the ceiling mocked our cries.

Afterwards, we knew that God Almighty had carried us through those dark times. We knew that the tears coursing down our cheeks were not only ours, they were also the tears of our Redeemer Jesus Christ, who still weeps today as He wept at Lazarus' tomb.

But in the teeth of the tragedy, we could hardly understand that we had merely joined the ranks of millions of sufferers who had gone before us. This happens to other people, this happens to stronger people—we can't bear this! This isn't the life we knew!

Is that faithless, unbelieving, carnal? When people blinded by tears dig among the rubble in the basement of their lives trying to find a foundation, does God chide them? When John sent his disciples to ask Jesus if He really was Jesus Christ the Lord, did Jesus condemn him?

No . . . instead, He said, "Verily I say unto you, Among them that are born of women there hath not risen a greater than John the Baptist: notwithstanding he that is least in the kingdom of heaven is greater than he."

When you ask God, "Are you who I thought you were? Are you real? Are you out there?" you are at the place where John the Baptist was. You are where thousands of God's servants have been. Your cry is very like the one that Jesus uttered on the cross: "My God, my God, why hast thou forsaken me?"

God had not forsaken Jesus! The prophecy in Psalm 22 assures us, "For he hath not despised nor abhorred the affliction of the afflicted; neither hath he hid his face from him; but when he cried unto him, he heard."

God did not forsake Job. He did not forsake John the Baptist. He did not forsake Jesus Christ. And He has not forsaken you.

Remember the story of Elie Wiesel in Chapter 8? In the crucible of horrible suffering he decided that either there was no God or He was weaker than man. In his mind, his former God swung from the Nazi scaffold, choked to death by reality.

Don't let your perception of reality murder your God and your soul. Don't let bad things consume your faith. Don't let tragedy turn your life to ashes. That is exactly what Satan wants to happen.

Jesus Christ did not come to erase the effects of the Fall on earth. In fact, He tells us, "In the world ye shall have tribulation." The same verse assures us that in Him we can have peace—not because He is planning and doing all that happens in the world, but because "I have overcome the world."[2]

Jesus Christ began a triumphant spiritual deliverance from the Fall for all who would believe on Him. In that deliverance, He did not violate His own rules. The earth is still fallen; and the soul that sins shall still die. But He gave eternal salvation to all who come to Him. He decreed, before there was a Satan and before there was a Fall, that the innocent, perfect Lamb of God could die to save the guilty.

---

2. John 15:33

In all your suffering, He is caring and weeping. In any tragedy, He is able to do more than you ask or think. In spite of any wrong choices you have made, He is able to redeem you to the uttermost.

What is your comfort?

In tragedy and suffering, you come to God with burning issues on your mind. You want to know what God is doing, you want to know why He allowed this to happen, you want to know that something good is going to come out of your grief.

But instead of giving you those answers, God says to you as He did to Job, "Let's look at the big picture. Can you make the deer have their fawns?"

And, like Job, you feel ignored.

Yet to understand the big picture—the war between Satan and God and the absolute truth of God's final victory—is the greatest comfort you can have in suffering. Don't feel ignored when God leads you to the big picture.

The idea that everything that happens to me is in the plan and will of God, and is woven by His hand in the tapestry of my life, is without Biblical support. The devil, other people, and our own carnal wills sew many things into our lives. So why are we so desperate to see the other side of the canvas?

The sight would not satisfy. Those details would not bring us the comfort we long for. The comfort we need comes from seeing our personal situation in relation to the big picture of God, Satan, and the war of the worlds.

The big picture is far more important than my situation. It is what helps me to make sense out of my situation.

Are we still sad? Yes. So is God. Are we still unsatisfied with the evil of the world and the effects of the Fall? Yes. So is God.

But are we satisfied with the big picture? Are we satisfied with the final disposition that God will make? Yes! So is God!

This view does not make your personal grief trivial or inconsequential. In fact, it makes your tragedies more consequential, because it fits them into the eternal picture of God versus Satan. It frees us from the self-focus of seeing tragedy as a situation between God and me. It leads us to the truth that tragedy hurts so badly because it is Satan's strike against God and you and me—the image-bearers of God. The tragedy that comes to you is also, in God's viewpoint, a tragedy.

God is not planning and willing bad things for you. God is preparing eternal good for you. In the end, God will

- remove all bad things,
- right all wrongs,
- judge all sin,
- save all repentant people, and
- avenge all innocent suffering.

All good will be with God, its Creator, forever. All bad will be with Satan, its author, forever.

Study Questions

1. What Bible characters inspire you to suffer faithfully?

2. Why do we tend to think that our suffering should result in future success or a great story?

3. Discuss how to avoid confusing the reason for suffering with the results of suffering.

4. Why is understanding the big picture the greatest comfort we can have in suffering?

"Be ye also patient; stablish your hearts: for the coming of the Lord draweth nigh" (James 5:8).

"And blessed is he, whosoever shall not be offended in me" (Matthew 11:6).

"Who in the days of his flesh, when he had offered up prayers and supplications with strong crying and tears unto him that was able to save him from death, and was heard in that he feared; Though he were a Son, yet learned he obedience by the things which he suffered; And being made perfect, he became the author of eternal salvation unto all them that obey him" (Hebrews 5:7-9).

"For in that he himself hath suffered being tempted, he is able to succour them that are tempted" (Hebrews 2:18).

"In all their affliction he was afflicted, and the angel of his presence saved them: in his love and in his pity he redeemed them; and he bare them, and carried them all the days of old" (Isaiah 63:9).

"For whether we live, we live unto the Lord; and whether we die, we die unto the Lord: whether we live therefore, or die, we are the Lord's" (Romans 14:8).

"And God shall wipe away all tears from their eyes; and there shall be no more death, neither sorrow, nor crying, neither shall there be any more pain: for the former things are passed away" (Revelation 21:4).

Magnificat anima mea Dominum!

Appendix

Is Permissive Will
a Biblical Term?

For centuries, theologians have used the terms *permissive will* and *perfect will*[1] to describe God's actions. They have taught that everything that happens in the universe must happen in one of these two modes of God's will. Augustus H. Strong explains this teaching as follows.

> All human acts, whether evil or good, enter into the divine plan and so are objects of God's decrees, although God's actual agency with regard to evil is only a permissive agency.
>
> No decree of God reads: "You shall sin." . . . He simply decrees to create, and himself to act, in such a way that you will, of your own free choice, commit sin. God determines upon his own acts, foreseeing what the results will be in the free acts of his creatures, and so he determines those results.[2]

---

1. *Perfect will* is also called *causative will* or *directive will*.
2. *Systematic Theology* (Valley Forge, Pa.: Judson Press, 1993 reprint of 1907 edition), p. 354.

The terms *permissive will* and *perfect will* come from classical theology as Strong here explains it. Those terms and their accompanying theology has led many people to believe the following.

1. God is sovereign.
2. Because #1 is true, God allows no being to thwart God's will.
3. Together, #1 and #2 mean that everything we see is in God's will.
4. The sum of #1, #2, and #3 is that God wills everything that happens.
5. Since God wills everything that happens, and the Bible teaches that God is good and righteous, it follows that everything that happens is good and righteous in some way.
6. Because #5 clearly contradicts many Biblical principles, there is now the insurmountable problem of understanding why and how God does things that His Word clearly says are evil. Here classical theology chalks up this contradiction to the mystery and incomprehensibility of God, while still insisting that everything that happens is determined and caused by God's will. Obviously holy and righteous things are called the *perfect will* of God, and obviously wrong and evil things are called the *permissive will* of God. It is insisted that there is no third category; *nothing* can happen *outside of* God's will.

The keen Bible student will notice that theology goes wrong in point #2 in the list above, with the result that all the remaining points in the list contain error.

Now, lets go back to the question about the term *permissive will*. I did not use it in this book for three reasons.

The origin and use of the term in classical theology is unscriptural.

In classical theology, *permissive will* does not mean "what God allows." Nor does it mean "what God allows but does not like." It means "what God creates, causes, and determines, even though He says He hates it."

Using *permission* and *will* together is confusing.

To *permit*, in the sense that God permits evil, is to allow, it. To *will*, on the other hand, is to deliberately choose, or to decree or dictate with deliberate intention.

In the "allow" sense of permit, *permit* and *will* are too different to be used together. How does God (or you) "allow will" something? That is nonsensical.

Beyond the "allow" meaning, *permit* carries the strong connotation of consent, license, or authorization. None of these terms correctly describe God's relationship to sin.

God blessed us with personal wills, so that we can choose Him and His will. That design means that we can also choose against Him. He *allows* us to choose against Him, but He does not *consent to*, *license*, or *authorize* this rebellion. Therefore, to say "God allows evil" is much closer to the Scriptures than to say "Evil is in God's permissive will."

The term confuses the clear, Biblical wording.

To claim that the carnal mind is operating in God's "permissive will" weakens God's statement, which is "the carnal mind is enmity against God: for it is not subject to the law of God, neither indeed can be."[3]

The Bible says that God's will is that all men be saved. So it clouds the truth to say that sinners are living in His "permissive

---

3. Romans 8:7

will." His will is the opposite of what they are doing, and they are not in it.

The Bible says that people can resist the Holy Ghost[4] and can resist truth.[5] God allows such rebellion, but He does not will it.

In **His will or** *out* **of His will**

The Bible says many things such as God "will have all men to be saved" and that He is "not willing that any should perish." So, there are:

> *(a)* actions and events in God's will (things that God wills and causes),
>
> and
>
> *(b)* actions and events out of God's will (things that God does not will or cause).

It has been said that in the end, there will only be two kinds of people: those who say to God, "Thy will be done," and those to whom God says, "*Thy* will be done." Those who live outside of God's will have chosen to be there. God did not choose them for that place. But He allows them to be there if they insist.

In the life to come, we will be in God's presence or out of it. We can apply that simplicity to God's will on earth. If we are *in* God's will, we are His "obedient children, . . . holy in all manner of conversation."[6] People *out* of His will are walking "after their own ungodly lusts. . . . sensual, having not the Spirit."[7]

---

4. Acts 7:51
5. 2 Timothy 3:8
6 1 Peter 1:14, 15
7 Jude 18, 19

Scripture Index